THE HISTORY OF THE SHIH TZU

By

Gay Widdrington

The History of the Shih Tzu
by
Gay Widdrington

ISBN: 978-0-9564037-0-4

Published by Onslow Publications (*1 Onslow Gardens, London SW7 3LX, UK*) in conjunction with Writersworld Ltd

Illustrations by Christian Garforth-Bles

Editors: Dot Shewan, Gillian Pattinson

Layout: Dot Shewan

Copy edited by Brian Stanton

Cover designed by Charles Leveroni and Christian Garforth-Bles

Printed and bound by
www.printondemand-worldwide.com

www.writersworld.co.uk
Writersworld, 2 Bear Close Flats, Bear Close,
Woodstock, Oxfordshire, OX20 1JX, United Kingdom

The text pages of this book are produced via an independent certification process than ensures the trees from which the paper is produced come from well managed sources that exclude the risk of using illegally logged timber while leaving options to use recycled paper as well.

CONTENTS

ACKNOWLEDGEMENTS

I would like to say a very big thank you to all those who have helped to make this book a reality.

To my stepfather Francis Widdrington, who gave me so much support and encouragement.

To Gillian Pattinson for her tireless help with documents, photos and items that my mother had compiled. For although most of the material was there it all needed sorting. Gillian then passed everything on to Dot Shewan who took on the marathon task of typing it all out and doing the layout. The two of them both did a further edit before handing the finished work to Jennifer Murray to work with Writersworld.

Christian Garforth-Bles

Contributors:

Elizabeth Legl, A. Berggre, G-M Sveden-Hall, Eija Verlander, Irene Booth, Elizabeth Ross, M. Kjaer, P. Burema, R. Maraolo, M. Mery, L. Reynelt, D. Deppenmeila, Mrs Gurney, Tom Horner, Mr Edward Jones, John L. Shepherd, Joan Reeves, Liv. Klokstad, Börre Hasle.

FOREWORD

I will always remember my mother with her beloved Shih Tzus - tumbling, frolicking at her heels, or on her knee being loved, combed, top-knotted and detangled; they were her constant and faithful companions. My mother had Shih Tzus of many colours and sizes but she had a dream of having a pack of golden lion dogs, which she realised!

My mother died before she was able to put the finishing touches to this book. Her husband Francis Widdrington, my cousins Gillian Pattinson, Jennifer Murray and myself, decided to publish it as it is. We have added a few photos which we thought she would like. It has been my pleasure to see to the completion of this 'History of the Shih Tzu' on which she had worked so hard and lovingly, having invested an immense amount of work and research.

Elizabeth Ross wrote a tribute to my mother, which was published in the winter 2005 edition of the Manchu Shih Tzu Society Newsletter. She knew my mother very well and had Shih Tzus of her own, and I have included her memories here.

I am sure that my mother would have liked to thank all her contributors very much indeed.

Christian Garforth-Bles

GAY WIDDRINGTON

Gay Widdrington was Honorary Treasurer of the Shih Tzu Club in 1947 - 54, and Chairman of it in 1954 - 56.

In 1956 there was a meeting at Crufts to establish a club for the smaller type of dog. She was founder member of the Manchu Club. From 1956 - 64 she was Chairman of the Manchu Club, and from 1964 - 77 she was President. In 1977 she became an Honorary Life Member.

She was also Patron of the Shih Tzu Club of New South Wales with Sue Dobson and Patron of the Shih Tzu Club of Scotland. She was a Life Member of the American Shih Tzu and Honorary Member of the Finnish Shih Tzu Club.

A Breed Columnist for 'Our Dogs' and 'Dog World', she also wrote articles for the Manchu Newsletter (N.E. News), and the Shih Tzu Club magazine, and wrote articles for Home and Overseas.

She judged in her first Championship show in 1957 as a breed specialist, and made many trips in the 70's and 80's judging in overseas dog shows. Among her interests were genetics, colour breeding and pedigree research.

At Crufts 1851 - 84, Lhakangs were 3 times Best of Breed. Fourteen British Champions have been produced by her Lhakang Kennel and fourteen more Cruft winners had one or more parent Lhakang. Lhakangs are behind many of today's winners.

Mrs Widdrington retired as Judge in 1988 aged 72.

MEMORIES OF MRS WIDDRINGTON AND HER SHIH TZUS

In the early thirties Sir Douglas and Lady Brownrigg brought back from China several little dogs, named Tibetan Lion Dogs to distinguish them from Chinese Lion Dogs (Pekingese). Mrs Widdrington saw and fell in love with them when she visited Lady Brownrigg on Red Cross business and obtained from her a bitch puppy named Mee Na of Taishan.

Mrs Widdrington founded her kennel in 1939, choosing as her affix 'Lhakang', the name of a Tibetan temple reputed to be the oldest building in the world. During the war food was scarce so Mrs Widdrington's dogs shared her meat ration. As Shih Tzus increased, Mrs Widdrington accompanied Lady Brownrigg who visited many litters. She began to show her dogs, travelling by train, accompanied by her butler who helped with the dogs and their luggage. She was a founder member of the Shih Tzu Club and held the appointment of Treasurer. She bred and showed dogs and made up Champions, thereby becoming well known and respected. She published a Shih Tzu Handbook in 1971 and was invited to judge at Championship Shows including Crufts in this country and in many other countries.

Mrs Widdrington loved the smaller Shih Tzus, which began to appear in litters and helped to found the Manchu Shi Tzu Society for their benefit. She offered several dogs at stud, including a clever boy who used to manoeuvre large visiting bitches into a convenient position with their rear end against the bottom step of the dog-room staircase!

Mrs Widdrington did not continue with studwork but concentrated on what she loved best, breeding and raising puppies, especially gold ones - her favourite colour. In total she bred 122 litters and exported carefully chosen good quality puppies overseas. From her last litter in 1996, she sent two bitch puppies to Finland and a dog to Norway.

Mrs Widdrington felt great concern for Shih Tzus in trouble and supported Mrs Ann Cragg's rescue work in North East England and Scotland. To raise funds, she organised informal classes, races and fancy dress events.

Mrs Widdrington was very worried when umbilical hernias began to occur. She believed they were hereditary and tried to persuade owners not to breed from affected stock. She imported sperm from Norway and bred a hernia-free litter for her own kennel, but the Kennel Club refused to register them, not favouring artificial insemination especially from a foreign dog, and not being convinced that hernias were hereditary. The beautiful dog puppy from the litter went to wealthy people in the Channel Islands who were not concerned about the lack of Kennel Club papers. They wanted to collect him in their private plane but bad weather prevented it, so they sent a chauffer driven Rolls to bring him home.

In March 2005, Mrs Widdrington's life came peacefully to its end, at home with her husband and daughter and four of her elderly dogs. It is what she would have wished. Shih Tzu owners here and overseas will feel sorrow at Mrs Widdrington's passing and will treasure their memories of her. She was my dear friend for fifty years and I shall remember her always with love.

Elizabeth Ross, May 2005

THE SHIH TZU

Exotic and enchanting little beast,
From China's guarded treasury released.
A priceless pearl to far more dearly prize
Than porcelain and jade in wondrous guise
Of all the precious things that fortune buys,
That human hands create and minds devise.
Wherein a pure and living beauty lies,
And with a soul to love that never dies.

Behold a dog! Diminutive in size,
But much in little - valiant and wise.
As fanciful to unaccustomed eyes
As phantoms conjured of an opium feast.
Its head a flower, its limbs and body fleeced,
Yet titled Lion! Erstwhile, in the East,
Of emperor of talisman, of priest
The sacred Dragon-dog of the deceased.

Luxuriously long and dense its hair -
And lovely! Of a texture to compare
With chiffon, crisp but soft to feel. That flows
Voluminously round it everywhere,
And falls, full sleeves and trousers where it grows
Upon the limbs, to cover up its toes.
With undercoat as warm as wool to wear
In winter, yet not burdensome to bear,
But light as feathers wafted in the air.

A coat to brush and comb with loving care -
Each day - to keep immaculately fair.
That consummates it elegance of form,
But was designed to keep a creature warm
(far back in time, in wild Tibet) that goes
Thus well-equipped against the cold and storm.
With mask as well as cloak, to less expose
Its eyes to danger from the dust that blows
In blinding gusts and from the winds and snows.

As exquisitely fashioned as a rose,
But copying capriciously, instead
A feathery chrysanthemum in head.
That hangs its hair about its eyes but shows
The soft, perceptive jet of mouth and nose.
The shaggy petals out - and overspread,
Or fastened in a topknot - if one chose
For comfort - and so doing, to disclose
The gaze and intelligence of those
Twin spheres, so dark and lustrous in the head.

Its rounded head with breadth of brow, large-eared
With pendent hearts that mingle in among
Embellishing its chin a bushy beard;
Escaping from its mouth a rosy tongue
At times, in panting eagerness outflung,
And other times demurely disappeared.

Its body made in all its parts to please,
With length enough of back, the breast low-slung
Between the forelegs and the ribs well sprung.
The hindparts heavy in proportion - these
Not lion-like but bear-like. Smoothly swung
Its legs, though short, like little trunks of trees,
Grown straight and muscular. While full of ease
And lissomness its gait, wherein one sees
Expression of a spirit ever young.

CHAPTER 1
TIBETAN ORIGIN

A Chinese divinity mounted on a "lion-dog",
after a sketch by V. Burkhardt.

Although the Shih Tzu (pronounced *Shid Zoo*, and meaning 'Lion King') gained its name and present form in ancient China, its ancestors are known to have originated in Tibet, and to have existed in that country as prized 'holy dogs' from Tibet's first recorded history in the 7th Century A.D., when Srong-Srong-Tsan-Gampa introduced Buddhism. Buddhism reached Tibet in its Tantric form and was modified by local legend and belief into the form known as Lamaism, which was mixed with an earlier animist form of religion.

One of these beliefs, held by Buddhists to the present day, was that people who had erred in their previous life were re-incarnated in a lower form - that of an animal. In the case of the Tibetan monks, this was in the form of a 'holy' or 'lion-dog', kept in the temples and played an integral part in various religious rites.

The puppies were recognised by the fact that they were 'born wise'. These shaggy little dogs were said to be bred in the shape of a lion, the sacred animal of the Buddhists - for the Buddha owned a little dog which, at a word of command would turn into a mighty lion and he could ride upon its back.

The Buddha is frequently depicted riding on his lion in old Chinese prints and on statues guarding the entrance to temples. Thus a black saddle, centrally placed, was highly prized on account of the Buddhist association with the harnessed lion.

Tibetan civilisation began to take its distinctive shape in the reign of King Song-Tsan Gampo (7th Century) who encouraged the spread of Buddhism from India and at the same time introduced various arts and customs from China. In return, precious gifts were sent to China as tribute to the Emperor. It was very fitting that amongst these gifts were carefully selected breeding-pairs of 'lion-dogs' sent in homage to Wen Shu Manjusri, the Buddha God of Learning.

The Emperor of China was flattered to have the small beasts following him like the attendants of the Saint. But it was not until the Ch'ing (Manchu) Dynasty, (1643 - 1912) that the Tibetan 'lion-dog' really came into vogue in China. Dogs were sent to all the Ch'ing monarchs down to 1908, when the Dalai Lama visited Tzu-Hsi, last Empress of China (who was particularly interested in dog-breeding) and presented her with several specimens shortly before her death the same year.

Lion-dogs were often kept in upper class Tibetan households as family pets, and 'good-luck' symbols.

3

CHAPTER 2
JOURNEY FROM THE ROOF OF THE WORLD

Considered by Tibetans to be the oldest house in the world.

The plateau of Tibet goes up to 16,000ft., and these fun-loving little dogs would make the long journey from Lhasa, in the highlands of Tibet down to the capital of China, Pekin, near sea level.

The journey from Lhasa to Pekin is over 2,000 miles and the 'lion-dogs' would accompany the caravans of yaks, mules, sheep and goats who carried loads of wool, hides, borax and amethysts. The pack animals would pick their sure-footed way over wild and mountainous country, fording rivers, crossing difficult ravines often covered with snow and ice, enduring cutting winds by day and bitter cold after sunset. The difference between night and day temperatures could be as much as 80 degrees.

They would travel through the great grasslands of north-east Tibet, over the pass called 'Mountain of the Moon and Sun' which separates Tibet from China, down to the hot plains of China until the gilded roofs of the temples and palaces of Pekin came into view at the end of the journey.

ON THE MARCH: LHASA TO PEKIN

The journey might take up to ten months and puppies would grow up on the way and have puppies themselves - the bitch probably whelping in a scraped-up hole in the corner of a tent at night. The puppies, when tiny, were carried in the pouched robe or 'shuba' of one of the Tibetans, next to the skin for warmth, and the mother would feed them during halts on the march. The dogs were fed on rice, dried meats and offal. Older puppies and dogs would ride in baskets on the backs of mules or scamper alongside, playing and barking on the march.

The 'lion-dogs' were used in the caravanserais to alert the rather slower huge and ferocious Tibetan Mastiffs who would kill if attacking a marauder. The 'lion-dogs' were always the first to bark and it was necessary for the stranger, if approaching a caravan, to shout ahead so that the mastiffs could be tied up.

CHAPTER 3
LIFE IN THE PALACE

Tibetan "lion-dog" in Chinese Art.
After the sketch by V. Burkhardt.

On arrival in Pekin, the 'lion-dogs' were graciously presented as fitting tribute to the Emperor, and ensconced in the Imperial Palace in the care of a host of eunuchs who were famed in the art of dog-breeding. Life must have been very soft and different to that which the tribute dogs had known previously, and bears witness to their incredible adaptability - a characteristic they show to the present day.

Here they were kept in a sumptuous pavilion with marble floors, situated 'behind the Ten Thousand Years Hill, where silk was dried in the sun'. They were taken for daily outdoor exercise and given regular baths. They were also taught to do various tricks. They shared the Royal Kennels with the Pug and the Pekingese (the latter being the 'lion-dog' of China).

The eunuchs vied with each other to produce the most beautiful specimens for the Emperor and his ladies. Symbolic colours and markings were highly prized, and no Tibetan 'lion-dog' must be more than 12lbs. in weight to find favour in royal circles. "Let the lion-dog be small" was one of the royal edicts. Gold, the imperial colour of

China was highly favoured, although well-marked parti-colours of every hue were cultivated. A white blaze on the forehead - "the holy mark of Buddha" was greatly treasured in parti-colours, and also a white tip to the tail. Body colour could be solid, banded or 'flowery'.

The boy Emperor Pu-Yi, who succeeded to the throne of China in 1908, aged 2, with his Lion-Dog (Shih Tzu).

To maintain the desired 'lion-like' proportions, the skilled eunuchs would occasionally cross the Tibetan 'lion-dogs' with the Chinese 'lion-dogs', i.e. the Imperial Pekingese, and in this way the Shih Tzu became shorter in face and leg than the Lhasa Apso, and with a most endearing blend of character - brave as lions, yet personal and loving, independent yet devoted companions, and truly wise as befits 'incarnations' of human beings!

It is also thought that the Maltese Terrier, which arrived from the Byzantine Empire in China during the T'ang Dynasty (618 - 907 A.D.), may be an ancestor of the Shih Tzu.

The Dowager Empress of China, Tzu-Hsi, walking her dogs in the grounds of the Summer Palace, Pekin (Circa 1880).

She is accompanied by her Lady-in-Waiting and a Eunuch.

Tzu-Hsi, famous last Empress of China, who reigned supreme at the end of the Manchu Dynasty, was particularly interested in breeding dogs and would pay a daily visit to the Royal Kennels. Her lady-in-waiting, the Princess Derling, records how the eunuchs would put the dogs through their tricks which they loved to do, and the dogs obeyed the Empress implicitly. The 'Old Buddha' would examine the dogs carefully and give advice on breeding.

The Dowager Empress of China, Tzu-Hsi, inspects a litter of Shih Tzu puppies bred in the Royal Kennels of the Imperial Palace, Circa 1880.

The Dowager Empress of China, Tzu-Hsi, seated on her throne, with some of her Lion-Dogs (Shih Tzus). Some of them are small 'Sleeve Dogs'.

No pedigrees were kept as we know them, but particularly beautiful specimens were painted by court artists on parchment scrolls which were used to inspire future breeding operations. One such scroll depicts a parti-coloured Shih Tzu with the caption, "From Tibet and very rare; its character is that of a human being". During the reign of the Empress Tzu-Hsi there were seldom less that 100 dogs in the Palace.

"Sent from Tibet as a present to the Emperor of China. Its temperament is that of a human being". (Collier).

Painting from an illuminated Imperial dog-scroll, used as a guide in the breeding programme at a time when no pedigrees were kept.

The Lion-dogs in the Palace were sometimes clipped to look like lions. (Rees Encyclopaedia, 1890).

CHAPTER 4
THE LION MOTIF IN CHINESE ART

There is much symbolism connected with the cult of the 'lion-dog' in the art of ancient China. The lion motif was greatly revered due to its many connections with the legends and tales surrounding the Buddha and the Saints, which had tremendous appeal to the Chinese mind. The actual animal - the lion - was not indigenous to China; hence the fancifulness of many of the works of art, and somewhere along the line the lion became identified with the 'lion-dog', in Tibet as well as in China. Thus the 'lion-dog' became a symbol of courage and it is in terms of these qualities that the motif appears, often in exquisite detail, in a wide field of works of art.

A Tibetan Lion-dog
(Shih Tzu Kou)
sketched in China by
V. Burckhardt.
"Hua Yah" - Flowery Duck.

The 'Lion-dog' appears, therefore, on an infinite variety of Chinese objects - from massive beasts carved from stone, guarding a temple, to delicate silken embroideries. There are 'lion-dogs' (or kylins) in silver and gold, bronze, jade, ivory and alabaster, fashioned in pottery or exquisite paintings on porcelain.

Lion-dogs in lacquered wood, Pekin.

The Shih Tzu type can be differentiated from the Pekingese type by the beard and whiskers and often with bumps on the head denoting a top-knot (Pien-ji).

CHAPTER 5
THE DEVELOPMENT OF THE SHIH TZU IN CHINA

Chinese lettering Shih Tzu K'ou "lion-dog".

Although Shih Tzus existed in the Imperial Palace under the puppet Emperor, Pu-yi, as late as 1928, breeding to type really languished after the death of the old Empress, Tzu-Hsi in 1908.

Stock became scattered abroad, smuggled out of the Palace and sold by the eunuchs to Chinese noblemen or presented as gifts to important foreign visitors. After this time, and up till the end of the 1930's much confusion arose as to the correct form and name of these dogs. Outside the Palace, the Shih Tzu and Apso types which existed in China at that time were all lumped together and called indiscriminately by the following names:

- o Tibetan Lion-dog
- o Lhasa Lion-dog
- o Tibetan Temple-dog
- o Tibetan Holy-dog
- o Lhasa Terrier
- o Ha-pa'rh Kou (pet-dog)
- o Tibetan Poodle
- o Shih Tzu Kou (lion-dog)
- o Tribute dog
- o Long-haired lion-dog
- o Shock-dog

This was at a time when there was no control system of registration for dogs in China - few pedigrees were kept and there seemed very little co-ordination between owners, either Chinese or European.

The China Kennel Club, Shanghai, was formed in 1923, but it was not until 1930 that the first class was scheduled at a show for this type of dog, under the name of Lhasa Terrier or Tibetan Poodle. The judge, Mr. A. de C. Sowerby, had a difficult task as there was absolutely no standard to go by and he urged ceaselessly that this type of dog be put on a proper footing in China.

In February 1933, he wrote in the China Journal of Shanghai (of which he was Editor):

It is in our opinion that the Tibetan Lion Dog is the result of a cross between the Lhasa Terrier and the Pekingese, which has arisen out of the mixing of the two breeds both in Tibet and China, since the dogs of each country have been taken to the other from time to time by tribute envoys and officials. The cross in Tibet, that has been taken out of that country by way of India, has been called the Apso, while the cross in Peking has been called the Tibetan Poodle or Lion-Dog. Doubtless the Tibetan cross has more of the Lhasa Terrier in it, while the Chinese cross has more of the Pekingese.

In 1934, the Peking Kennel Club was formed and a class scheduled for 'Lhasa Lion Dogs'. A standard now existed, but the exhibits were said to deviate greatly from it, especially in size. In 1935, the Lhasa Lion Dog proved one of the most popular in the show, an amazing number of ribbons being won by Mrs. Kun Chin's small black and white bitch.

"Mo'er," Mrs. R. Laurenz' Lhasa Terrier dog (Shih Tzu), winner of the First Prize in the recent Dog Show in the China Kennel Club in this class.

(From "The China Journal" - Aug. 1930).

The breed continued to improve in China as the years went by. In 1936 the Lhasa Lion Dogs were judged at the Pekin Show by Madame Lu Zee Yuen Nee (author of the booklet The Lhasa Lion Dog (Shih Tzu) published by the Pekin Kennel Club). At this show, type was much more uniform and some exceptionally good specimens were exhibited. At the 1937 Pekin Show Contesse d'Anjou's Lhasa, named 'Shih Tso' was Best Non-Sporting Bitch, and Best Bitch in the Show. Unfortunately the Japanese occupation began later in 1937 and put an end to further dog shows.

THE LHASSA LION DOG

(1) Dragon eyes	Phoenix tail
Lion head	Tiger back
Bear torso	Elephant leg
Camel hoof	Owl face
Frog mouth	Movement like a gold fish
(2) Bell eyes	Incense burner front
Ju Yi (scepter) nose	Pen brush holder legs
Kneading board body	Feather duster tail
Tassel like hair	Charcoal heater mouth
Palm leaf fan ears	
(3) Lin Tse nose	Chrysanthemum tail
Peony petal tongue	Plum blossom paws
Apricot eyes	Kwantung gourd ears
Water caltrop mouth	Water chestnut face
Rice teeth	

From Mdme Lu Zee Yuen Nee's book -
"The Lhassa Lion Dog (Shih Tzu)",
published in Pekin in the 1930's.

18

CHAPTER 6
THE CHINESE STANDARD

Three generations of golden Shih Tzu.

This colour was highly prized in China as it symbolised yellow, the Imperial Court colour.

The following is the Pekin Kennel Club's official standard for the Shih Tzu (Lhasa Lion Dog) dated 1938:

LION HEAD

Long ears:	Heart-shaped (the longer the hair on the ears the better).
Long apron and pantaloons:	Long hair is difficult to get in hind-legs and all the more appreciated.
Size:	13-18 ins.

Weight:	10-15 lbs.
Height:	9-12 ins.
Eyes:	Large and clear (the hair should fall over them and cover them completely if possible).
Toes:	Well feathered; paws broad and flat.
Front Legs:	May be slightly bowed (controversy about this).
Hindquarters:	Slightly higher than back.
Hair:	As glossy as possible; apron and pantaloons wavy.
Skull:	Broad and flat.
Tail:	Well-plumed, carried gaily over back.
Colours:	All colours permissible, single and mixed. Tawny or honey-coloured highly favoured.

In January 1949, the Communists came to power in China and all dogs (being consumers of food) were destroyed. This ends the history of the Shih Tzu in China, and the scene shifts to the Western World.

CHAPTER 7
THE SHIH TZU IN THE WESTERN WORLD

Cover of Manchu Shih Tzu society newsletter.

The British Isles

Luckily by the time the Communists occupied China, the Shih Tzu was becoming well established in the Western World. In 1930 various Europeans connected with the Diplomatic Service decided to find specimens and take them back home with them.

General Sir Douglas and Lady Brownrigg bought a dog and a bitch, Hibou and Shu-ssa in Pekin and imported them to England, and Miss E.M. Hutchins imported Lung-fu-ssu and Mei-Mei into Ireland. Unfortunately the bitch, Mei-Mei was killed soon after leaving quarantine.

The three remaining dogs became the foundation of the breed in the British Isles and the basis of the famous 'Taishan' strain.

An early Apso bred in England in the 1930's.
The nose is distinctly longer, the eyes smaller and the head narrower than the
Pekin-bred Shih Tzu.

At the same time Colonel and the Hon. Mrs Eric Bailey imported several dogs of similar type from the borders of Tibet, and at first these importations were classed together under the name of 'Apso' which meant 'shaggy or goat-like'.

But when they and their offspring appeared together in the show-ring for the first time in 1934, they differed so much in appearance that it was decided to divide them into two quite separate breeds; those with longer noses and legs were name 'Lhasa Apso' and those which came from Pekin, and had developed shorter, rounder heads and shorter legs, were called 'Shih Tzu' (meaning 'Lion'), by which name they had been known colloquially in China.

*Yangtze of Taishan, born in quarantine from
the first imported pair to England - Hibou and Shu-ssa.*

From this time onwards the two breeds drew steadily apart, although to this day an occasional specimen is seen in the show ring which resembles the other, and it is always important to preserve the distinct characteristics of each to prevent confusion between these two long-haired breeds.

In 1934, the Shih Tzu was recognised in the Non-Sporting Group in 'Any Other Variety', and Lady Brownrigg was granted permission to register the club under the title of 'The Shih Tzu Club', under the Presidency of the Countess of Essex. For many years to come there was healthy rivalry between Apso and Shih Tzu Breeders, often referred to as 'the war of the noses'.

Early breeders stressed that the Shih Tzu was a hardy active dog, capable of good country walks, and that it was 'neither a terrier nor a toy'. In character it was bold and assertive, loving and yet very independent and often with a clownish sense of humour, which made it enjoy learning tricks.

In 1933, a male was presented to H.M. the Queen Mother, then Duchess of York, by Mdme. Kauffman, wife of the Danish Minister in China, who had brought three back to Scandinavia the previous year. This black and white dog, Choo-Choo was bred to Lady Langman's bitch, Fu of Taishan, and the Royal Family kept a daughter, Mau-tse, and for many years Shih Tzus were to be seen at the Royal establishments. This line is to be found in all extended pedigrees of British stock today.

Princess Elizabeth, (later Queen of England) with her sister, Princess Margaret Rose, and their "Lion-Dog" Ching, a descendent of Chou.

An occasional specimen also went to the U.S.A. Some confusion again arose, as although there were two separate breeds in the British Isles, for some time all dogs of this type imported into America were re-classified as Apso, although they came over with Shih Tzu pedigrees and Export Certificates.

At this time there were Apso breeders in U.S.A. who were anxious to prevent the recognition of the Shih Tzu. This practice of re-classification was finally stopped in U.S.A. in 1952, and Shih Tzus were no longer classified as Apsos. But it was not until 1969 that they were officially recognised and then in the 'Toy Group', which dismayed many British breeders, as they felt this would open the way to change essential and cherished characteristics. The universally adopted English standard had been accepted on the Continent of Europe in 1934, by the F.C.I. (Fédération Cynoligique Internationale) but the Apsos made slower progress here, and their standard was not published until 1960.

By the end of 1938 well over a hundred Shih Tzus had been registered by the English Kennel Club. Championship status was granted in 1940, but this lapsed during the war years. It was not until June 1949 that Lady Brownrigg's beautiful bitch, Ta-shi of Taishan became first breed Champion at Blackpool Championship Show. The Shih Tzus had made their own effort towards the war - their combings were sold for £1 for the Red Cross, and knitted up into comforts for the troops!

At the end of the war, in 1945, Shih Tzu stock was very low, but there was enough to bring about a steady increase, and new importations soon arrived from abroad.

In the next 35 years registrations rose from only two to over 2,000 per annum, making the Shih Tzu the third largest in the Utility (formerly non-sporting) group by 1980, after Miniature and Toy Poodles, with 29 sets of C.C's at all the main championship shows.

Lady Brownrigg was Secretary of the Shih Tzu Club from its foundation in 1935 until 1954. She then continued as President until her death on 15th April 1969, nearly 40 years after she and her husband had first introduced the breed to England. Two days before she died she heard the news that the Shih Tzu was to achieve official recognition by the American Kennel Club the following September. However they were to be classified in the Toy Group, a move against which she had always campaigned.

1937: A memorable group.
L to R - Hibou, Yangtze, Tzu-Hsi and Shu-ssa.

Hibou and Shu-ssa were the Brownrigg's first imports from
China, and the foundation of the Taishan strain.

In 1962 a second breed club was recognised by the English Kennel Club - the Manchu Shih Tzu Society. One of the aims of this Society was to give latitude to a smaller type of Shih Tzu, more in keeping with those bred in the Imperial Palace, Pekin, which were under 12 lbs. There was a tendency for the breed to increase in size with each generation, perhaps due to a better diet. Under pressure from this Society a revision in the standard was brought about allowing the lightest permissible weight down from 12 lbs. to 10 lbs.

In 1952, a Pekingese-cross was introduced into British stock by Miss E.M. Evans, a famous Pekingese breeder. This was to improve various points and was done under Kennel Club control. Each generation was published in the Kennel Gazette until the fourth and 'pure-bred' generation was reached, which was eligible for Class I registration. Although not everyone agreed about the advisability for the cross, this line proved very popular and soon spread to all British

Kennels, and produced top winners here and overseas. A small dog, Fu-ling of Clystvale, went to Sweden in 1959 where he produced numerous Champions. Here a smaller type of dog was thriving, classified in the Toy Group.

In 1952 a Pekinese cross was introduced into the breed in England to improve various points. This is a first-generation bitch.

During the 1960's a boom in exports to U.S.A. began, but to be accepted there Shih Tzus had to be seven generations from the cross. This popularity was partly brought about because many British breeders were breeding selectively for a smaller, higher quality dog.

The English Standard of Points, with only slight modifications has been accepted all over the world, including the wide weight range. However, the British pride themselves on the fact that it is far harder to make up a Champion here than in any other country, and this maintains a high standard in type and conformity. British Shih Tzus are always owner-handled in the ring, and never trimmed.

Mee Na of Taishan (bred by Lady Brownrigg).
Pups by Ch. Choo-ling, a grandson of Royal "Choo-choo", 1947.
Pups: Yen Mo, Chen Mo and Lindy-Lou.

Re-union in the Western World:

The Venerable Akong Rinpoche with his two puppies Pema and Tashi and his older dog, Sing Frug, (all obtained in England) at the Samye-Ling Tibetan Centre, Dumfries-shire, 1968.

CHAPTER 8
BLOODLINES IN THE BRITISH SHIH TZU

All present day stock in the British Isles descends from twelve imported dogs. Of these, seven came from China 'pedigree unknown'. In the past, the English Kennel Club permitted such dogs to be given Class II registrations on the recommendation of a specialist judge, but this did not of course guarantee genetic purity. Over a dozen other dogs were imported, usually from China or Scandinavia, but these lines did not continue.

The Communists came to power in 1949, and after this it was impossible to obtain Shih Tzus from the mainland of China. Sad tales were heard of dogs being stoned to death as they 'ate the food of the people'.

The original bloodlines in the British Shih Tzu are as follows:

HIBOU, d.	1930	Imported from Pekin by Gen. Sir Douglas and Lady Brownrigg.
SHU-SSA, b.	1930	Imported from Pekin by Gen. Sir Douglas and Lady Brownrigg.
LUNG-FU-SSU, d.	1930	Imported from Pekin by Miss E.M. Hutchins (Eire).

CHOO-CHOO, d.	1930	Given to H.M. The Queen Mother by Mme. Henrik Kauffman, wife of Danish Minister to Norway. Parents from China.
TASHI of CHOUETTE, b.	1938	Imported from Canada by the Rt. Hon. The Earl of Essex. Parents from China.
MING, b.	1939	Imported from China by Lt. Gen. Telfer-Smollett, Lord Lieutenant of Dunbartonshire.
ISHUH TZU, b.	1948	Imported from Shanghai by Lt. Gen. Telfer-Smollett.
WUFFLES, d.	1948	Imported from Tientsin by Mr. and Mrs. Fraser Buchanan.
MAI-TING, b.	1949	Imported from Shanghai by Mr. and Mrs. Rowland Morris.
HSU-LI-YA, b.	1952	Imported from Hong Kong by Mr. R.P. Dobson.
PHILADLEPHUS SUTI T'SUN OF ELFANN, d.	1952	A Pekinese-cross introduced by Miss E.M. Evans. Four generations had to elapse, mating back to the pure, before this line could be registered as 'pure-bred'.
JUNGFULTETS JUNG-MING, d.	1959	Imported from Sweden by Mrs. M. Longden.

CHAPTER 9
THE SHIH TZU IN SCANDINAVIA

EGM

Scandinavia has played a most important role in the history of the breed, since three Chinese dogs were brought to Norway in the early 30's and founded world-renowned strains in the Scandinavian countries.

The first Shih Tzu were imported into Norway by Mrs. Kaufmann, the wife of the Danish Minister in China. After his return to Europe, Mr Kaufmann was transferred to the Danish Legation in Oslo, so the three imports were registered with the Norwegian Kennel Club.

It is fitting that the acquisition of the first aristocratic Shih Tzu was highly dramatic. It is said that Mrs. Kaufmann saw some small long-haired dogs when walking along a street in Peking. They were to be burnt - probably in connection with a religious ceremony, perhaps a funeral. Mrs Kaufmann begged the Chinese to show mercy to the dogs and finally she took one of them with her. She was so enchanted by the breed that she made up her mind to acquire two more specimens. In a letter to Lady Brownrigg she recounts the difficulties she had experienced in obtaining the small specimens she wanted. It took her a year and a half to find a male, having seen dozens of coarse dogs. Two years later she found a second bitch. The three dogs were:

- The black and white dog, Aidzo, born in Peking in 1930.
  Sire: Law Hu.
  Dam: Lun-Geni.

- The brown bitch Leidza, born in the Imperial Palace in 1928.
  Sire: Chin-tai.
  Dam: Wu-hi.

- The black and white bitch Schauder, born in Shanghai in 1931.
  Sire: Aidzo-Huh.
  Dam: Hu-luh.

Mrs. Kaufmann considered Leidza an extremely beautiful specimen - in fact better than the other bitch, Schauder, who according to her own opinion was a bit high on the legs. In Norway the dogs were registered as Lhasa Terriers. At this time there was great confusion about the small Tibetan and Chinese breeds and they were all lumped together under the name Lhasa Terrier. In 1939 the Norwegian Kennel Club asked Lady Brownrigg for advice and the breed was finally registered as Shih Tzu.

One of Aidzo's and Schauder's best-known progeny was Lingen. Despite the very high degree of inbreeding the breed did not show any signs of weakness. Lingen's granddaughter N & S Ch. Vokenlias Shih-Tzu was mated four times to her sire N Ch. Law Hu II and twice to her son Yun Toy from a litter sired by her father (!). Her offspring had a tremendous influence on the whole breed.

breeds in Sweden. In March 1969 the Swedish Shih Tzu Society was founded, officially recognised in 1981.

In 1955 the breed was introduced into Finland by Mrs Irja Kunnari, Tornio. The first imports were the bitch Shepherds Yen-Psung, born in 1954, and the dog Shepherds Hien Kiang, born in 1953. They were bred by Mrs Hauffmann, Sweden. In all Scandinavian countries the Shih Tzu is judged in the Top Group.

Little Hornblower from Major Hasle's Boreas Kennels.

CHAPTER 10

THE FINNISH SHIH TZU IN A NUTSHELL
by Eija Verlander

In 1955 the first Shih Tzu was introduced in Finland by Mrs I. Kunnari and since then the breed has gained more and more fanciers. In Finland the breeders are almost all exceptional people who have their own professions outside home and the breeding is only a dear and demanding hobby for them. This is fortunate for the breed, as it is certainly one of the last to be able to live kept in kennels. Yet this doesn't mean that the breeders did not take their hobby seriously - on the contrary - with only 2-3 bitches in the family they plan their breeding programme very carefully. The Shih Tzu Club of Finland was founded in 1971 and has nowadays over 300 members. The yearly registrations have been between 160 and 200 during 1970-1979. In 1981, 174 Shih Tzu were registered.

The first breeder with importance to the Finnish Shih Tzu was Mr Artti Sepp. The first litter in his CAPELLA fame saw daylight in 1961. The dam was his import from Norway, Chow-Ah-Ling. Since those early years the co-operation between Norway, Sweden and Finland has been active, as it still is today. Mr Sepp also imported some dogs from England. One with much influence on the breed was Int. & Nord Ch. Edsville Fu Yung of Elanzo from Miss Martin. This black and white dog was the first Shih Tzu in Finland to gain an international title. He also sired many champions, among them Int. & Nord Ch. Genius Pei-Pik, Sf & S. Ch. Marella Tatzang and Sf. Ch. Capella Cu-Ling. In the early 1970's Mr Sepp imported several dogs from the Liliencrons kennel owned by Mrs B. Larsen-Rosvall in Sweden, such as Sf, & S. Ch. Liliencrons Lord Maurice and Int. & Nord Ch. Liliencrons Lady Capella.

Nowadays there is only occasionally a litter in the Capella, but Mr Sepp is still a keen shower - his latest import from Sweden from Mrs Fossenius, Int. & Nord Ch. A-Abracadabra (Liliencrons-line) was the Top Winning ST in Finland in the years 1980 and 1981. Many champions have been born with the Capella name - such as Sf. Ch. C. Taitzung, Sf. Ch. C. Philomena, Sf. Ch. C. Tit-Tzu. Int. & Nord Ch. C. Fu-Hi - just to mention a few. Int. & Nord Ch. Capella Jim was the Top Winning Shi Tzu in Finland and the winner of the Club Speciality in 1978. He is owned by Mr. H. Mutanen (MARELLA), who continued the line and has also bred champions.

Another early breeder was Mr Pekka Vissi with the kennel name Kauhakuusen. He imported his foundation bitch Nord Ch. Nankings O-Fe-Lia (a daughter to Sch. Fu-Ling of Clystvale) in 1963 from Sweden. She was for example a winner of 7 CACIBS and dam to such champions as Sf. Ch. Kauhakuusen Tzu-En-Lai and Kauhakuusen Tsang-Sha. In 1966 Mr Vissi imported Sf. Ch. Lochranza Khan Du from England, bred by the Misses McMillan and Coull. This dog became a successful stud and sired many champions e.g. Int. & Nord Ch. Kauhakuusen Wen-Tai, Int. & Nord Ch. Scedessan Da-Zaza and Sf. & S. Ch. Kauarmaan Käli-Tsou. In 1968 O-Fe-Lia and Khan Du had a litter of five and in this litter there were such winners as K. Charles (imported to France) and Sf. Champions K. Cajus, Casse and Camilla. The last mentioned was a very successful show bitch even at her veteran age. She won the Club Speciality in 1976 and 1977.

In 1971 Mr Vissi imported Sf. Ch. Law Hu van de Blauwe Mammouth from Holland, who also sired many champions - Sf. Ch. Attalos Littlecherry, Sf. Ch. Attalos Littlecamilla, Sf. Ch. Sirklahden Fixidea and Sf. Ch. Kauhakuusen Mammouth to mention a few. It is a great pity though, that this knowledgeable breeder did not continue his breeding because of his demanding profession. Yet his Shih Tzus lived long lives in the Vissi family as much loved pets.

The History of the Shih Tzu

Mrs Sirkka Lahdenperä (SIRKLAHDEN) purchased her first Shih Tzu from Mr Vissi in '68, Sf. Ch. Kauhakuusen Casse. She was a dam to such champions as Sirkladen Fixidea and Sirklahden Kadri-Lee. In 1974 Mrs Berggren from Sweden imported a Shih Tzu dog from England, Int. & Nord Ch. Kurt's Boy of Lansu. This magnificent dog (line bred to Ch. Golden Heidi of Elfann) has had a great influence on the breed in Sweden, but also in Finland. Mrs Lahdenperä mated Sf. Ch. Sirklahden Kadri-Lee to this dog and this outcross produced such champions as Sirklanden Pa-Ya and Po-La, both now dams to champions.

To strengthen the line Mrs Lahdenperä imported a Heidi-son Sf. Ch. Lansu Tribute to Heidi from England, from Mr & Mrs Hoyle, and Sf. Ch. Anibes Pee Wee Peony, a daughter to "Kurt's Boy" and Nord Ch. Elfann Golden Meadow Sweet, from Mrs Berggren in Sweden. With these dogs Mrs Lahdenperä has succeeded very well indeed, e.g. gaining the award of "Top Shih Tzu Breeder of the Year" in 1980 and 1981, during the years this award has been granted by the Club. She has bred many champions e.g. Sf. Ch. S. Titta-Po, Sf. Ch. S. Yu-Chin, Sf. Ch. S. Zeus and Sf. & S. Ch. S. Wu-Ling, the last mentioned being BOB at the Club Speciality in 1981 and 1982.

As this story is meant to be only a short introduction of the Finnish Shih Tzu history, I have only mentioned those breeders with most importance considering the present representatives of the breed. Yet there is one breeder still to be mentioned - Major B. Hasle from Norway with his Boreas Shih Tzu. The first from this kennel arrived in 1977 imported by Miss Pakarinen - Int. & Nord Ch. Boreas Mei Hsi Ch'iao - a daughter to the sire of many winning champions: Nord Ch. Lhakang Jolyon from Mrs Widdrington. B. Mei Hsi Ch'iao was the Top Winning Shih Tzu in Finland 1979 and in her first litter (with a Jolyon grandson) produced 2 with International titles and 2 with two-country titles. Also some other Shih Tzu have been imported from this successful kennel, e.g. Nord Ch. Boreas Elfann Lodestar and Sf. & N. Ch. B. Chinese Peregrine, both sons to Elfann Golden Hopeful from Miss Evans.

At the present time the Shih Tzu is enjoying a very favourable period - this can be seen in their growing numbers where there are often between 30-50 Shih Tzu in any one show today.

CHAPTER 11
THE BLENDING OF BLOODLINES

With the importation of more English stock into the Scandinavian countries, some kennels have achieved notable success in blending these two bloodlines.

Int. & Nord Ch. Kurt's Boy of Lansu (English import) winning Stud Group at Stockholm International show in November, 1979, out of 60 all-breed entries.
Here he is pictured with five Champion sons and daughters.
He is handled by his owner, Anita Berggren, (Anibes Kennel).

The 'Anibes' kennel, owned by Anita and Kurt Berggren in Sweden has produced some beautiful dogs since a decade or so ago. Their stud dog, Int. & Nord Ch. Kurt's Boy of Lansu (English import) has produced some outstanding offspring to Scandinavian bitches, or those with already blended inheritance. He was top winning stud dog all-breeds in Sweden, 1977, 1978 and 1979. The Berggrens have imported three English bitches, the most outstanding being Eng. Int. and Nord Ch. Bellakerne Suki Sue, multiple Best-in-Show winner, and top winning Toy in Scandinavia in 1978 and 1979, also second top-winning dog all breeds in Sweden 1979.

*'Chinny' - Chin-Pao of Elfann
and her baby.*

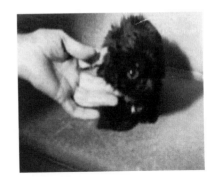

Major Börre Hasle (Boreas Kennel) has imported good stock from leading English Kennels (including Elfann, Lansu, Whitethroat and Lhakang). He has also achieved great success in combining bloodlines, and his black and white and gold and white stock alternate well. His foundation stud dog, Nord Ch. Lhakang Jolyon, has produced over fifteen Champion descendents.

Ch. Boreas' Imperial Beauty Spot by Lansu Teatime ex. Lansu Starlight Time, bred and owned by Major B. Hasle, Norway, who has imported nine outstanding British dogs and used these importations thoughtfully and judiciously for the improvement of his own breeding program, which has resulted in 16 champions.

Several other Scandinavian breeders have also imported stock to strengthen their bloodlines, and another successful kennel is that of Mrs. Engstrom who has imported the outstanding stud dog, Nord. Ch. Whitethroat Mr. Wu. He has produced some beautiful progeny either to pure Scandinavian bitches, or to the progeny of Ch. Kurt's Boy of Lansu, and vice versa.

This interbreeding has brought more substance to the Scandinavian Shih Tzu who are now going ahead on a very strong basis, but it is to be hoped that the charming Scandinavian type will not be lost, as both strains have a lot to offer the other.

CHAPTER 12
BREED STANDARD OF THE SHIH TZU

GENERAL APPEARANCE

Sturdy, abundantly coated dog with distinctly arrogant carriage and chrysanthemum-like face.

CHARACTERISTICS

Intelligent, active and alert.

TEMPERAMENT

Friendly and independent.

HEAD & SKULL

Head broad, round, wide between eyes. Shock-headed with hair falling well over eyes. Good beard and whiskers, hair growing upwards on the nose giving a distinctly chrysanthemum-like effect. Muzzle of ample width, square, short not wrinkled, flat and hairy. Nose black but dark liver in liver or liver-marked dogs and about one inch from tip to definite stop. Nose level or slightly tip-tilted. Top of nose leather - should be on a line with or slightly below lower eye-rim. Wide open nostrils. Down pointed nose highly undesirable, as are pinched nostrils. Pigmentation on muzzle as unbroken as possible.

EYES

Large, dark, round, placed well apart but not prominent. Warm expression. In liver or liver-marked dogs, lighter eye colour permissible. No white of eye showing.

EARS	Large, with long leathers, carried drooping. Set slightly below crown of skull, so heavily coated they appear to blend into hair of neck.
MOUTH	Wide, slightly undershot or level. Lips level.
NECK	Well proportioned, nicely arched. Sufficient length to carry head proudly.
FOREQUARTERS	Shoulders well laid back. Legs short, and muscular with ample bone, as straight as possible, consistent with broad chest being well let down.
BODY	Longer between withers and root of tail than height at withers, well coupled and sturdy, chest broad and deep, shoulders firm, back level.
HINDQUARTERS	Legs short and muscular with ample bone. Straight when viewed from the rear. Thighs well rounded and muscular. Legs looking massive on account of wealth of hair.
FEET	Rounded, firm and well padded, appearing big on account of wealth of hair.

TAIL	Heavily plumed carried gaily well over back, set on high. Height approximately level with that of skull to give a balanced outline.
GAIT/MOVEMENT	Arrogant, smooth-flowing, front legs reaching well forward, strong rear action and showing full pad.
COAT	Long, dense, not curly, with good undercoat. Slight wave permitted. Strongly recommended that hair on head is tied up.
COLOUR	All colours permissible, white blaze on forehead and white tip-to-tail highly desirable in parti-colours.
WEIGHT & SIZE	4.5 to 8.1 kgs. (10 - 18 lbs.). Ideal weight 4.5 to 7.3 kgs. (10 - 16 lbs.). Height at withers not more than 26.7 cm (10½ins.). Type and breed characteristics of the utmost importance and on no account to be sacrificed to size alone.
FAULTS	Any departure from the foregoing points should be considered a fault and the seriousness with which the fault should be regarded should be in exact proportion to its degree.
NOTE	Male animals should have two apparently normal testicles fully descended into the scrotum.

*Another name for the Shih Tzu is
"Chrysanthemum Dog",
as its moppy head can look like a big
double chrysanthemum.*

CHAPTER 13
COMMENTS ON THE SHIH TZU STANDARD

The Standard of Points paints a word picture of the ideal Shih Tzu within a certain framework, and anyone hoping to cultivate an "eye" for a good specimen should study this standard carefully and apply it not only to the outward appearance, but to the actual structure of the dog under the coat.

HEAD

This is a most important point, as correct head structure gives the Shih Tzu its unique appeal. The broad round head should make two spheres - the rounded skull and the square muzzle. The skull should be wider from side to side than from front to rear. The large, dark eyes should be set wide apart, with more than an eye's width separating them, and show as little white in the corners as possible. Beautiful dark eyes with a warm expression complete the endearing face, and have the effect of drawing the onlooker's affection.

The actual nose-placement can make or mar the whole expression; this should be about one inch from tip to stop. A rough guide would be under 14 lbs, ¾"; 14-16 lbs, 1"; over 16 lbs, 1¼". Muzzle square and short. The bridge of the nose should be level or slightly tip-tilted, with a definite stop. Once you get a "down" nose, it leads to other undesirable points such as too much length, a snipey muzzle, narrow head, and small or almond eyes. A long-nosed dog is more likely to be overshot, leading to a weak chin, another point which spoils expression. If the nose-placement is correct, then the top rim of the nose-leather will be on a line or slightly below the lower rim of the eyes.

The leather should be broad and the nostrils well open. The upper lip should be neither too long nor too short, but roughly the same depth as the nose leather, and there should be a strong chin. A nose which is too squashed in perhaps with over nose wrinkle is incorrect, and will cause discomfort to the dog as there will not be room to accommodate the fall of hair either side of the muzzle, which will tend to lie across the eyeball and cause irritation, or the eye-ducts will be badly placed and fail to drain properly, causing a tear-stained face, soreness and discolouration.

The ears should have long leathers, set slightly below the crown of the skull, and carried drooping, which gives a pleasing frame to the face.

MOUTH

Scissor-bite undershot is ideal, with a wide even jaw. There should be six incisors (small front teeth) top and bottom; two canines top and bottom either side; twenty-six molars, seven on each side of the lower jaw, and six on each side of the upper jaw. Total: 46 teeth.

In a short-faced breed it is not unusual to have only four incisors top and bottom (this can lead to a narrow jaw) and a molar missing top and bottom on each side, or sometimes the molars are slightly turned in the gum to make room for them all. Few judges will stop to count all of a dog's teeth but will be satisfied if the incisors and canines are intact.

It sometimes happens that Shih Tzus have two incisors on the bottom jaw placed behind the others, a feature which the Chinese fancied, but which Westerners do not!

NECK

This is not mentioned in the standard, yet it can affect the whole balance of the dog. It should be neither too stuffy nor too long, but of the right length for the dog to get its head up smartly on its shoulders, with a nice crest. Ideally the head and tail should make almost equal elevations either end. A heavily-coated dog will have a good ruff or mane, but under this one should be able to get one's hand easily round the neck, except in a very tiny specimen. An outline with a long reachy neck, and the tail lying too flat or screwed, gives quite the wrong impression.

FOREQUARTERS

In a short-legged dog with a "broad deep chest" it is very difficult to get a completely straight front, and this can be easily seen in other short-legged breeds with smooth coats. However, the American standard does call for a "straight front", whereas in the British Isles, where the standard was first drawn up, a slight curve in the upper forearm is expected to accommodate the rounded body. This curve should be felt but not seen in a heavily-coated specimen. In Scandinavia, where the original strain was more lightly built and higher on the leg, a "straight" front is also called for.

Whatever the difference of opinion of build, the front paws should face forward, the shoulders should be firm, and the heavy fall of coat should hide the curve in the upper fore-arm. A perpendicular line from withers should pass through forefoot. There should be "ample" bone in the legs, and paws should look "massive" on account of the wealth of hair.

BODY

This should be sturdy and well-coupled. The "coupling" is the distance between the withers and hip-bones which should not be overlong. Nevertheless the dog should be oblong and not square, the length from withers to root of tail being longer than the height at withers.

The following is a rough guide to body proportions:-

Weight	Height at withers	Length: Withers to root of tail	Chest to Ground	Ratio
12 - 14 lbs	8 - 10"	3-4" longer than height at withers	3 - 5"	2:3 or 3:4

The body is not waisted nor "cut up" but more or less tubular.

The topline should be level, and this is sometimes difficult to get, especially if the back is long. The dog may dip at withers due to loose shoulders or a bowed front, giving a back which slopes downwards from rear to front. Stifles which are too straight can accentuate this.

The Chinese cultivated a "down-in-front" look which they considered to look like a "lion rampart", and since the Peking Club permitted a bowed front, this structure must have been common in China before the breed came to the West, so that it is not surprising that it crops up today. A back which slopes the other way, downwards from front to rear, is a bad fault and seldom seen. A roach back is also a bad fault and gives the dog a miserable look.

WITHERS

Unless the dog is of a rangy build, the withers will not be excessively laid back as in a terrier or a whippet, etc. and the slope of shoulder should be sufficient to give adequate angulation between the shoulder-blade and the upper forearm. This angulation is essential for good front action otherwise there will be a tendency to goose-step or paddle, or the elbows will protrude and the dog will be pin-toed.

HINDQUARTERS

These should be well-muscled, with good angulation and hocks well let-down to give the necessary drive. The bone should feel fairly thick but not cloddy. The hind-legs should look parallel when viewed from the rear, neither bandy, too close, nor cow-hocked.

FEET

Of good size and well-padded; usually there is hair between the toes. Feet should feel firm and muscular, not flabby or splayed. Small cat feet are a fault.

DEWCLAWS

The Chinese considered that dew-claws on all four feet were the sign of a perfect dog! Our present day Shih Tzu often have only two on the hind-legs or none at all.

Dew-claws can be removed in the nest at 3-4 days old by the vet, but this is not essential. If left on, however, care should be taken to cut them back regularly, otherwise they may form a circle and cut into the flesh.

TAIL

"Curved well over the back, carried gaily; set on high". This means that the tail set-on should be fairly high, and that the tail-leather should be curved well over the back in a loop or "tea-pot handle". A tail which lies flat on the back, falling too much to one side or in a screw is wrong and spoils the whole balance of the dog. Of course the long plume often falls to one side or the other, but the actual tail should curve centrally over the back.

COAT

The coat is the Shih Tzu's glory, and for show purposes, every hair should be treated as precious. There should be an undercoat and long topcoat, so that the dog has a slightly "bouffant" appearance. Care must be taken not to rake out the undercoat on a show-dog. The coat should be luxurious, long and dense, but the actual texture can vary somewhat with different colours, and can be likened to human hair. A very soft, silky or woolly texture, which mats easily and absorbs dirt and wet like a sponge, is to be avoided. Rather the coat should have a certain toughness and resilience. A straight or slightly wavy coat is much smarter than one with too much curl or frizz, which is anyway a fault. Profuse head-furnishings (giving the true "Oriental look") and long hair on legs and paws completes the picture of the dog "all in one piece". After a puppy is 4-5 months old, the hair on top on the head should be tied up with a small rubber band.

COLOUR

All colours permissible, solids or parti-colours, ranging from blue-black to grey or fawn, and from rich red or apricot to pastel honey and champagne. The pastel shades can be very glamorous, providing the pigment is dark, whereas black/white or red/white parti-colour is more striking. Liver is a permitted colour, but it is essential that the eye-rims, nose and muzzle are a really dark chocolate. Strong lasting colours should be aimed for in blacks and red/golds without the "fading" gene, which turns colours wishy-washy. A true brindle colour is one in which the black hairs mingle with the brown or red, and go right to the roots.

GAIT

The legs of a sound Shih Tzu should appear to move straight, or parallel to each other coming and going, though, as mentioned previously, the heavy fall of coat may hide a slight bend in upper forearm. Pads should face forward, and the dog should move with a good flowing action, throwing its hind legs out well behind it and showing the up-turned pads. This needs a good bend of stifle and firm muscular condition. It may have a slightly rolling gait. Poor muscle tone can quite alter the appearance and movement of the dog, causing loose shoulders, bad topline, or sway-back, and a dog down on its pasterns. The dog should not move "wide" either front or rear, nor should the legs be too close together or cow-hocked (knock-kneed) behind.

SIZE

The weight range (9-18 lbs.) gives a lot of latitude. The Shih Tzu does vary in size, and there can be considerable difference in one litter. The middle weight of between 12-15 lbs. is a good size to aim for, with dogs slighter larger than bitches. The dog should feel surprisingly heavy when picked up. In China a smaller dog was favoured - it had to be under 12 lbs. to be approved in the Imperial Palace, and often tiny but perfect specimens appear in litters with above average intelligence, as if thrown back to "sleeve-dog" ancestors. Height at withers can be difficult to assess depending on depth of coat, and how the dog is standing. A dog of 15 lbs. or under would not normally stand higher than 9-10½" at withers if solidly built and correctly proportioned in other ways. Dogs of 18 lbs. and over can be coarse and untypical and are rarely seen in U.S.A., where Shih Tzus are classified in the Toy Group. A smallish high-quality dog is very acceptable for show, but as the standard points out "Type and breed characteristics are of the utmost importance and on no account to be sacrificed to size alone".

A dog of "quality" has the bearing and expression, plus the excellence of conformation and coat which makes him look a real aristocrat.

CHAPTER 14
FAULTS AND HEREDITARY PROBLEMS

The Shih Tzu on one side of its pedigree shares common ancestry with other small Tibetan breeds so that it is essential to keep them quite distinct. It is only in the Western world that separate standards were drawn up for each, and this was in the 1930's - not so very long ago. Although the Shih Tzu normally breeds true to type, it is not surprising if occasionally a puppy appears in a litter which grows up to look more like a Lhasa Apso, Tibetan Spaniel, or small Tibetan Terrier.

A dog with a narrow skull, snipey muzzle and almond eyes (which often go together), will resemble a Lhasa Apso in appearance, especially if it has a long neck and screw tail to complete the picture. If it also has long legs, then it will look more like a small Tibetan Terrier. Sometimes "flat-coats" appear in a litter which grow up to look more like a Tibetan Spaniel with similar feathering.

Lastly there is the Pekinese or Chinese Lion Dog which we know the Chinese incorporated into the Imperial Shih Tzu (or Tibetan Lion-Dog) every few generations to produce the Shih Tzu type as we know it today. This cross was again introduced in England to counteract various undesirable tendencies. Thus exaggerations of a pekey type must also be guarded against. The most obvious of these are smooth faces, ultra short noses with overnose wrinkles, protuberant eyes, obviously bowed front legs with toes turning out, and tail lying flat on the back. Sometimes a puppy will have more the peke type of coat - very fluffy in infancy, but going right out of coat in adolescence, and then growing in with more the peke texture and featherings. Typically, a Shih Tzu puppy should coat up steadily to adulthood, and not go drastically out of coat at any stage of growth.

The History of the Shih Tzu

We are fortunate that in the Shih Tzu we have a dog with no excessive exaggerations which in themselves can lead to unsoundness and ill health. We are told that all breeds of dogs which have been adapted by man will, if left to themselves revert to the basic canine, the jackal or the wolf, so that breed characteristics must constantly be bred in. The Shih Tzu is a breed which can "bolt away" like an unruly weed, if bred carelessly, becoming large, rangy, leggy and wild of temperament.

The cosmetic faults of the Shih Tzu, which really spoil the appearance, are pale or light eyes, pink patches on nose, muzzle and eye-rim. This broken pigment is more likely in parti-colours that have a lot of white on their faces. If the pigment does not fill in by 12 weeks, then you have cause to worry. Sometimes pale coloured dogs will have "dudley" noses, i.e. noses which turn pink in the centre in cold weather or when out of condition. Seaweed powder can help both these conditions. In parti-colour the eyes sometimes show too much white in the inner corners - the wider the white flash and muzzle, the more this is likely to occur, as if the lack of pigment extends to the eyeball. This can be seen in other parti-colour breeds such as Boxers and Japanese Spaniels. In the latter it is a necessary feature in their standard as the look of 'astonishment' is considered desirable! Also it can be seen in parti-coloured cattle. Thus it appears to be linked more to markings than bloodlines, but the condition isn't inevitable. You rarely see it in solids or dogs with dark faces.

However in Shih Tzus the white flash and muzzle are highly prized in parti-colours, and it is a matter of degree whether it is a serious blemish or not. It is more inherent in some strains than others, and the aim should always be a dark eye, which really fills the socket.

Other faults which are not mentioned in the standard, (which is there to describe ideal conformation) are those which affect the wellbeing of the dog. In short faced (brachycephallic) breeds, it is very common for puppies in the nest to develop pinched or tight nostrils at about 3 weeks old. If these are very tight, then the pup cannot breathe and suck at the same time and will drop off the nipple, fade and die, unless watched carefully and handfed. Usually this condition clears up when the second teeth are cut. The seriousness of this complaint is a matter of degree and records on all pups should be kept - two dogs which have suffered badly in infancy should never be bred together. With careful selection it is desirable and possible to breed this condition out, for every puppy has a right to draw fresh air into its lungs and this is important for healthy development, and to prevent a concave ribcage.

Monorchidism (only one testicle descended into the scrotum) is another heredity fault which needs watching. Usually a puppy will be entire by three months. Although monorchids are usually fertile, it is unwise to breed from them, or from bitches who throw this fault. It can also lead to dogs of very uncertain temperament.

Hernias are a hereditary problem, although the bitch can help to cause these by pulling too roughly on the cord at whelping time. Hernias can be umbilical, inguinal (in the groin) or scrotal. Again it is a matter of degree, as a puppy may soon grow out of a small umbilical hernia; inguinals can also disappear. Scrotals can be the most serious, as the dog may have to be castrated. The tendency for hernias runs more in some strains than others and it means that the stomach wall is too thin. It is perfectly possible to breed them out by wise selection.

TEMPERAMENT

The Shih Tzu has an excellent temperament and is good with children. He is active, lively and alert and very adaptable, and will usually see off dogs larger than himself. He is independent yet loyal and loving, and will usually take an intense interest in everything his owner does. He can also be very clever at learning tricks, although his independence can make him "do his own thing" if left to himself. When dogs kept for show live a confined life, the owner misses so much, as the dog never has a chance to develop his true character which can bring so much pleasure. Although the Shih Tzu has now spread all over the world, one rarely hears tales of a nasty-natured dog, which shows that all those who breed them have generally taken care not to spoil the character by breeding from nervous or bad-tempered dogs. For the healthy development of ones strain it is important to use good mothers and keen studs.

In breeding animals we have a big responsibility to take action and mirror what would occur in natural circumstances i.e. to breed only from animals which are sound in body and mind, and ensure that they go to the right sort of homes where they will be properly cared for. It is a natural instinct in wildlife to destroy deformed or weakly offspring and it is up to us to eliminate such animals from our breeding programmes to avoid future suffering. Domestic animals are at our mercy and their wellbeing is in our hands.

CHAPTER 15

SHIH TZU IN AUSTRALIA : 1954 - 1978

By John L. Sheppard

The Shih Tzu came to Australia in 1954, when English Bulldog breeders, Tony and Sue Dobson, established their 'Wawnehill Kennels' in N.S.W. The three dogs that came with them Pei Ho of Taishan, a black and white dog who had won two English C.C.'s, Wen Chin of Lhakang, a chestnut and white dog puppy, and the black bitch Chloe of Elfann; all became Australian Champions.

The Dobsons did much to promote the breed in Australia, with stock going to most States. From the original imports Mrs. Dot Avery founded her 'Newglen Kennels. She also had an imported dog at stud by the name of 'Lee Lisan of Lhakang'.

Stock from both these kennels formed the nucleus of what must be the most famous of kennels in Australia - Mrs. Gwen Teele's 'Geltree Kennels'. With most of the stock being closely bred on the original imports, Mrs. Teele decided that she must import, so in 1958 the black and white bitch 'Hia Nan of Snaefell', arrived to be followed in 1959 by the black and white male 'Ty Yung of Antarctica' - both became Australian Champions. With the valuable bloodlines the Geltree Kennels were on their way, with stock going throughout Australia, New Zealand, Singapore, the U.S.A. and Holland. In 1963 Mrs. Teele obtained a small grey and white dog from the U.K. He became Aust. Ch. Skoal of Eyeworth; this dog was a grandson of the Swedish imported dog 'Jungfultets Jung Ming'.

Without a doubt the most famous of the 'Geltrees' was Mrs Joan Reeves' outstanding black and white dog Aust. Ch. Geltree Ty Ching; not only was he a successful show dog but a prolific stud. He holds the honour of being the FIRST Shih Tzu to win Best Exhibit in Show All Breeds in Australia. Another outstanding Geltree worthy of mention is Mrs. J. Gaspero's black and white bitch Aust. Ch. Geltree Cheng Lui. This bitch was a consistent winner with numerous Group and In Show wins to her credit.

Due to the large number of imports in recent years I have listed them with colours and sex when known. Those on this list are those who have produced stock and can be seen in many pedigrees:-

N.Z. CH. YING KUO OF ANTARCTICA (U.K.) black and white dog.
AUST. CH. SAFFRON OF GREENMOSS (U.K.) mahogany and white bitch.
AUST. CH. CHIN WANG OF GREENMOSS (U.K.) gold and white dog.

LI KUNG LIN OF CHASMU dog.

Both are supposed to be golds.

TON FAN OF CHASMU bitch.

AUST. CH. KEYTOR CHRISTOPHER ROBIN (U.K.) black and white dog.
GREENMOSS GOLDEN GLORY (U.K.) black mask, gold dog.
AUST. CH. RIGNABEE OF GREENMOSS (U.K.) brindle and white dog.
AUST. CH. LHAKANG CHEN PI YU (U.K.) black mask, gold dog.
CROWVALLEY STYLUS (U.K.) gold sable and white dog.
TELOTA RAMA (U.K.) black and white bitch.

Due to a rabies scare in 1969, all imports were banned for several years, and breeders were obliged to use their own ingenuity, and dogs available. When the ban was lifted in the early seventies imports arrived from a number of different kennels in the U.K., and with the availability of a wider choice of stock, Australian Shih Tzu began to take their place amongst the world's best.

One of the first imports to set the pattern for big wins was Ch. Saffron of Greenmoss; she won B.I.S. All Breeds at COLOMEKE in

1970 under famous International All Rounder, Mr. W.G. Siggers. She was a good sized bitch with a magnificent head, producing a number of winners for Dr. Cunningham.

CHANSLYNE

MEE CANCAN

(Great Grand-daughter of CLEO)

Sire Aust. Ch. Chanslyne Taboo out of Chanslyne Mitzee (another class in group winner).

Pretty brindle and white, Cancan won bitch CC and Runner-up B.O.B. 1977 R.A.S. Spring Fair, Best Puppy Shih Tzu Club of N.S.W. 1st Show.
Her Dad was Res. CC at 1976 Spring Fair.
She needs only a few points more for her title.

The breed has won well in recent years, especially at the Royal shows. In March 1973 the seven months old bitch TSUYUNG SO SWEET SUM WUN was awarded Best Puppy Bitch in Show - 'Pussy', as she is known, went on to complete her title at 8 months; this black and white bitch was bred by Mrs. Bales, owned and handled by John Sheppard.

In September of that year Mrs. Bales won Opposite Sex Puppy in Show at Adelaide Royal with the black and white bitch TSUYUNG FAN CI MEI. 1974 saw the grey and white dog KAJABBI KRACKLES, owned by Mrs. L. Walsh, win Best Puppy in Show in Adelaide, and at the same Royal in 1975 the glamorous pale grey and white bitch SHEMARA AUTUMN LEAVES, owned by the Gardiners, accounted for Best Puppy in Show as well as Opposite Sex in Group. This bitch is still winning B.I.S. at major shows. Her most recent claim to fame would be her Best in Show win at the prestigious Victorian Shih Tzu Club's Championship Show, the judge being Mr. Tony Dobson of N.S.W., the original importer of the breed to Australia.

Another bitch that has a string of B.I.S. is King and Wood's CH. LOUANNE CHEN HSING. She is a small blackish grey bitch with a white chest - I believe that she is now retired.

In a field which has been dominated by bitches for some time, we now have males that are making their presence felt: Ch. Garaig Ko Ko - bred by Shirley Leach and owned by Paul and Julie Nash won Best in Show All Breeds in late 1977. He is a black and white dog who has won in the N.S.W. ring.

In February, 1978, Lhotse Sun Yat Sen, a black and white dog imported and owned by John and Lee Sheppard, won Best in show All Breeds at 13½ months of age. This makes him the FIRST imported Shih Tzu male to gain this award and one of the youngest.

We have been lucky with our show wins in N.S.W. In Victoria Joan Reeves keeps 'knocking on the door' with her 'Ch Tsuyung Fanci That' - he is a black and white dog with a number of Group wins to his credit and three Opposite Sex in Show All Breeds.

1978 - 1982 by Joan Reeves

The breed is now in a very strong position in the show ring. Though entries have not increased to any extent, the quality has been maintained, presentation is excellent, and Shih Tzu are taking out top awards at shows all over Australia, so the honours are not restricted to the few well-known exhibitors in New South Wales, Victoria and South

Australia. The many imports in the last few years have no doubt helped maintain the high standard in the breed, though some of the top winning stock goes back to the original bloodlines and those 'greats' of the early 1970's - Ch. Chin Wan of Greenmoss (U.K.), Ch. Saffron of Greenmoss (U.K.) and Ch. Keytor Christopher Robin (U.K.). Notable amongst these is Mrs. Pam Bales' Ch. TAO TING-A-LING (bred by Mrs. Loretta Walsh and sired by Ch. SHEMARA TALISMAN), one of the best known dogs in Australia today, a consistent winner of Best in Show awards over the past four years and sire of many of Australia's top winning Shih Tzu. Two of his sons - Mrs. Rosemarye D'Agostin's Ch. TILCHA LINK INTIME and Greg Royall's Ch. TSYUNG MING DYNASTY - are multiple B.I.S. winners and sires of winning stock, and his daughters, Mrs. Bales' Ch. JANJU COLOURED GOLD and John Glen's Ch. TSUYUNG PETIT POINT, won B.I.S. at the N.S.W. Shih Tzu Club's Championship Shows of 1980 and 1981 respectively.

The steady stream of imports has continued - they are far too numerous to list but the following are worthy of mention because of the impression they have made on the breed:

TAONAN LIESL (U.K.): This bitch unfortunately had a short life but numerous B.I.S. winners are descended from her.

TAONAN HUMPHREY (U.K.): Silver grey dog - Sire of B.I.S. winner Ch. TAO BOBBY DAZZLA and is the pedigree of many of today's winning stock.

Aust. Ch. GREENMOSS GOODNESS ME (U.K.): Black and white dog - A.B.I.S. winner and sire of numerous Champions.

Aust. Ch. CHING WUN OF GREENMOSS (U.K.): Black and white dog - A.B.I.S. winner.

Aust. Ch. SANTOSHA SHENENDOAH (U.K.): Sable and white dog - Son of Tom Tru of Lhakang and sire of B.I.S. winner.

Aust. Ch. CROWVALLEY MINERVA (U.K.): Brindle and white bitch - Mother of Eng., Braz & Int. Ch. CROWVALLEY POSEIDON, great grandmother of Eng. & Aust. Ch. Delridge Golden Gemini at Crowvalley (U.K.), and Wentrees Peregrine (U.K.): and in the pedigree of many of today's winners in Australia.

Aust. Ch. GREENMOSS GERONIMO (U.K.): Gold and white dog - Multiple B.I.S. winner and sire of winning stock.

Aust. Ch. KEYTOR M'LORD (U.K.): Gold and white dog - B.I.S. winner and sire of winning stock.

Eng. & Aust. Ch. DELRIDGE GOLDEN GEMINI AT CROWVALLEY (U.K.): Gold and white dog - Son of Eng. Ch. Crowvalley Pegasus, multiple B.I.S. winner and sire of winning stock.

Ch. WENTRES PEREGRINE (U.K.): Gold and white dog - Son of Eng. Ch. Crowvalley Pegasus. This young dog is a consistent in-show winner and sire of winning puppies.

Aus. Ch. Tao Bobby Dazzla is the pedigree of many of today's winning stock.

Aus. Ch. Wentres Peregrine (U.K.). Gold and white dog - Son of Eng. Ch. Crowvalley Pegasus.

Aus. Ch. Naichiu Alana.

Aus. Ch. Peking Tella Tale.

Amongst the locally bred Shih Tzu there have been many outstanding dogs and bitches and the future looks very bright with a lot of lovely puppies making their debut. It is impossible to mention all those who have excelled either in the show ring or as producers, but three 'firsts' are worth recording:

The History of the Shih Tzu

Mrs. Clay Hutcheson's Ch. PEKING PAN LU, a brindle and white bitch, was the first Shih Tzu to win a group award at the Melbourne Royal Show when she took out Best Puppy in Group in 1976; Mrs. Joan Reeves' Ch. TSUYUNG FANCY THAT, a black and white dog, was the first of his breed to win B.I.S. (All Breeds) in Victoria (1978); and the Gardiner's Ch. SHEMARA SHO-EM-HOW, a black and white dog, was the first Shih Tzu to win Best in Group at a Royal Show (Adelaide1981).

To date Australian Shih Tzus come entirely from British imports and are similar in type to top winners there.[*] The ancient Chinese would tell you that nothing in life remains constant, there is the Ying and the Yang…the Ebb and the Flow. Today we breed to a written standard; changes have been made and will continue to be made. But we, as breeders, should remember that with us lies the heritage of this ancient dog of China - not bred for its scenting ability, speed or obedience. This is the 'Shih' - the aristocrat of dogs…. With the heart of the lion and the intelligence of the scholar, always expecting an honoured place in the household as his birthright.

The sensation of 1981 was the gold/white bitch puppy, Ch. Erintoi Star Dust who won the Bitch C.C. and B.O.B. from the Puppy Class then went Best Puppy Bitch in show at the Sydney Royal under English judge, R.M. James. This bitch was U.K. bred, owned by Erintoi, and then sold to Shemara Kennels of Adelaide.

---

[*]From a paper read by Mr. M. Johnson, Chairman at the 1st seminar of Shih Tzu Club of New South Wales, 1978.

CHAPTER 16

WELL KNOWN MODERN BRITISH KENNELS
By Irene Booth

The sincere breeder has one desire - to aim for the near perfect dog. We are aware that complete perfection is an impossibility, but we do strive, through a study of blood lines, to improve our stock and to produce dogs of the highest quality. In Shih Tzus we are fortunate in having a number of dominant dogs and bitches who have passed on their excellence to their offspring. For that reason this survey will endeavour to map out the lines and families descending from certain prepotent dogs, starting with the Greenmoss kennel owned by Jeanne and Arnold Leadbitter.

The Greenmoss kennel was founded on Wyntoi, Lhakang and Elfann stock. Their well known Champion - Greenmoss Golden Peregrine of Elfann - made up in 1968, sired several litters of noteworthy stock before being exported to Italy and gaining his title there. Introduction of breeding stock from Brownhill and Telota lines further strengthened this kennel. Their very prepotent stud dog, Ch. Greenmoss Chinki of Meo (sired by Choo T'sun of Telota, and bred by Mrs. V. Reynolds) produced numerous litters of high quality stock bearing his own stamp, and is behind most of the winning strains today.

More recently, the influence of Ch. Greenmoss Glory Bee can be seen in many of the winning solid golds and gold/whites. His daughter, Ch. Greenmoss Me-in-a-Bonnet was top winning Shih Tzu in 1980. Their Greenmoss Bees Knees (top winner 1981) and Harry Baxter's Ch. Ragoosa Golden Raffles, now belonging to Paul Sorenson, were both sired by him. He was one of the top winning studs in 1982, with seven of his offspring winning nine C.C.'s., another daughter by a later litter - Ch. Surely Bee of Greenmoss - was Best of Breed at Crufts 1983. Another son of Chinki's - black/white Ch. Greenmoss Chinki's Fling - has also proved a strong stud force and is behind numerous show winners today. In 1982, five of his offspring won seven Championships.

Greenmoss dogs have been exported world-wide, in particular to Australia, where Australian Ch. Greenmoss Geronimo has been used widely at stud. Other well known dogs from this kennel 'down under" are Australian Chs. Saffron of Greenmoss, Ringabee of Greenmoss and Chin Wun of Greenmoss.

A recent export to Sweden is Greenmoss Tit-for-Tat, gold/white, now a Swedish Champion who is proving a big winner and excellent producer.

Having lived many years in Lancashire, the Leadbitters have now crossed the Pennines to Yorkshire. They have been active in forming the new Northern Counties Shih Tzu Society. Arnold resigned from Chairmanship of the Manchu Shih Tzu Society in 1983.

The Lansu Shih Tzus, owned by Tom and Sylvia Hoyle, began with the acquisition of a black/white dog, Mista of Greenmoss in 1966, who won several first prizes. Two years later they obtained the first of four beautiful "Elfann" bitches. These were Ch. Golden Heidi of Elfann, Ch. Golden Summertime of Elfann, Ch. Elfann Golden Posy of

Lansu and Ch. Elfann Golden Joyful. Miss E.M. Evans was in her last years of active breeding, and the Hoyles felt it important to preserve this good line for posterity, line breeding to the famous sires Ch. Golden Peregrine of Elfann and Ch. Greenmoss Chinki of Meo.

The result has been numerous national and international champions out of surprisingly few litters, including the well known English sires Lansu Eastertime of Elanzo and his son Elanzo Gold Digger. Perhaps the most famous of all is Int. and Nord. Ch. Kurt's Boy of Lansu, owned by the Anibes kennel in Sweden and 3 years running top winning stud dog all breeds there (1977, 78,79). Lansu dogs have made a valuable contribution to the breed in many countries including the U.S.A., Australia, Norway, Sweden, Finland, Germany and Ireland. During Tom's long terminal illness, activities had to be curtailed for several years, but in 1982 Sylvia (now Mrs. John Rawlings) started breeding again with a litter out of Lansu Golden Melody by Lansu King's Ransom.

Amongst those that have made their mark in various countries, either as breeding or show stock are:

- o   Am. Ch. Lansu Blossom Time

- o   Lansu Show Time (U.S.A.)

- o   Lansu Starlight Time for Boreas (Norway)

- o   Lansu Tea Time for Boreas (Norway)

- o   Int. & Nord. Ch. Lansu Heidi's Fair Lady

- o   Finnish Ch. Lansu Tribute to Heidi

- o Am. Ch. Lansu Magnolia Time

- o Am. Ch. Lansu Winter Time

- o Irish Ch. Treasure from Heidi

- o English Ch. Lansu Fragrant Cloud

- o German Ch. Lansu Philanderer

- o Australian & New Zealand Ch. Karens Gold Strike of Lansu

- o Int. & German Ch. My Choice of Lansu

Les and Stephanie Williams, who live in Wales, keep a small kennel of top quality stock. Their first Shih Tzu was purchased from Ethel Lewis (Siwel) in 1969. This was Crowvalley Siwel Sing Lu who carried the Antarctica, Snaefell and Telota lines. She was mated to Ch. Jen-kai-ko of Lhakang (bred by Mrs. Widdrington and owned by Eunice Fox). This litter produced Crowvalley Yameeto (black/white), one of the most prepotent bitches in the breed.

Her first litter was by Elfann Golden Sunrise of Tricina (owned by Eric and Tina Carter) and grandson of Greenmoss Chinki, producing the gold/white Ch. Crowvalley Tweedledum, top winning Shih Tzu in 1976. The second litter, by Ch. Zeus of Bridgend (owned by Mrs. Thornton) who was a Chinki son, produced Ch. Crowvalley Minerva, herself a good producer in Australia (one of her offspring in Australia: Ch. Tilcha Mouchy Mouch). Yameeto's third litter, sired by Hyning Yessir (owned by Tom and Sheila Richardson) produced Canadian Ch. Crowvalley Llewelyn, and her fourth litter, sired by Ch. Ya Tung of Antarctica, produced Mrs. Irene Booth's Ch. Bowstones Shan Tung, top winning Shih Tzu 1978. It can be seen that Yaneeto produced consistently good offspring from different lines. Prior to her move to Australia, Crowvalley Minerva was mated to her half-brother, Ch. Tweedledum. This produced Ch. Crowvalley Poseidon who was exported to Mr. Tuck-Schneider in Brazil where he became a Grand Brazilian and International Champion.

Mr Tuck-Schneider also acquired a gold/white Tweedledum daughter, now Brazilian Ch. Nokes Lu-Li. She is out of a daughter of Ch. Dominic of Telota. Ch. Poseidon was bred to Tricina Kay prior to his export, and this litter produced Ch. Crowvalley Pegasus, who is the sire of Australian and English Ch. Delridge Golden Gemini at Crowvalley (breeders Ms Budd and Wilson), who are siring quality stock in Australia. At home another of Pegasus' sons, Ch. Crowvalley Peter Pan at Crowvalley is a well known winner and producer. In 1982 Pegasus was one of the top studs - nine C.C.'s being won by two of his progeny. This kennel has concentrated on producing sound dogs with profuse coats.

Amongst the up and coming young owner-handlers is Wendy Greves of South Wales, who with her mother's help has produced some exceptionally good and well-presented dogs. Her first was Ch. Telota Simon Chen, a grey/white son of Ch. Dominic of Telota, bred by Mrs. Olive Newson. Their Ch. Wentres Jay Cee Valencee (sired by Ch. Crowvalley Tweedledum) went Best of Breed at Crufts in 1981 and 1983. Others from this kennel are home bred gold/white Wentres Scaramouche (by Crowvalley Pegasus) now a Junior Warrent holder, and Wentres Peregrine, now an Australian Champion in the hands of John Glenn.

Another of our young owner-handlers is June Papps. Her first Shih Tzu, Ch. Tricina Tai Haku, gained his title in 1974. This small gold/white dog with profuse coat is a son of Elfann Golden Sunrise of

Tricina (bred by Eric and Tina Carter). At ten years of age he won the Reserve Championship at the Manchu Shih Tzu Club Championship Show. One of his sons, now being shown by June, is Ch. Eastern Promise of Honeylee.

Tom and Sheila Richardson of the Bellakerne kennels, who came into the breed in 1970, specialise in black/white, though their first dog, Hyning Yessir was gold/brindle and white. Although an excellent producer, his show career was cut short due to an eye injury. Their foundation bitch was the beautiful black/white Patsy Do of Hyning, who subsequently became a Champion and has produced four champion offspring - Ch. Bellakerne Zippity-Do, Ch. Bellakerne Inca-Do (both by Yessir), Ch. Bellakerne Melissa-Do (retained) and Ch. Bellakerne Zoe-Do (owned by Mrs. Thelma Morgan) and Australian Ch. Chinki-Do (owned by Mr. Bonney). These last three were sired by Ch. Greenmoss Chinki's Fling, following the Richardson's policy of keeping closely to the Greenmoss strain. Their first Champion was Ch. Bellakerne Suki Sue, gaining her title in 1978. Her sire was Crowvalley Yenesei (litter brother to the dominant bitch Crowvalley Yameeto) and she was out of Bellakerne Button, a daughter of Patsy Do. Suki Sue became a Swedish Champion in the hands of Anita Berggren and had a spectacular show career, but unfortunately died before she could be bred.

The Antarctica kennels of Ken and Bettie Rawlings are known to all Shih Tzu people. Since 1945 their dogs have won more than 270 Championships in the breed. However, lately they have spent more time showing their Tibetan Terriers. A mention must be made of the great dog Ch. Ya Tung of Antarctica, born in 1969 and producer of five champions. The two recent ones are Irene Booth's Ch. Crowvalley Shan Tung, top winning Shih Tzu 1978, and Dorothy Gurney's Ch. Darrall's Felicity, top winning Shih Tzu 1980. Mrs. Todd's Trisula, bred to the Antarctica strain and in 1978 made up Ch. Trisula Chioh Koh of Antarctica (who also contains Telota breeding).

Mrs. Olive Newson has had to give up breeding due to indifferent health. However, her breeding lines are still playing a prominent part in today's dogs. Their latest Champion, Dominic of Telota, sired six champions and is a grandsire of several promising younger dogs.

John and Sylvia Carter (Montzellas) have kept to the Telota line. Ch. Montzellas Tsi Chou is a black/white son of Ch. Dominic who sired Ch. Montzellas Chink to Chen, also black/white. The Carters are unable to attend many shows but always bring out something good.

Michael Harper has a good foundation bitch, Ch. Telota Anouska, bred by Olive Newson and is showing some good stock from Telota and Antarctica lines.

Mrs. Hoare bred another daughter of Ch. Dominic - Ch. Gorseycop Splendid Summer, grey/white, who gained her title in 1981, owned and handled by Mrs. Anne Pickburn. She is the daughter of Sheila and Charles Duke (Janmayen) who have been associated with the breed for many years, Charles being Vice-President of the Shih Tzu Club.

Ellen Johnson (Keytor), in partnership with her daughter Susan, based her kennel mostly on Greenmoss breeding. Her first Champion was the lovely black/white Ch. Keytor Sweet Charity, winning her first certificate at just 11 months old and another the next week, gaining her title in 1973. She is sired by the famous Ch. Greenmoss Chinki of Meo. A litter brother, Australian Ch. Keytor Christopher Robin, was top Shih Tzu in Australia two years running and sire of nine Champions. In 1974 Ch. Keytor Midas gained his title (sire Ch. Chin-ling of Greenmoss). Two bitch Champions followed in 1981, Ch. Keytor Dreamer, black/white (sire Ch. Greenmoss Chinki's Fling) and Ch. Keytor Trische Trasche, a solid gold by Ch. Greenmoss Glory Bee. This kennel has exported a number of dogs, including Australian Ch. Keytor M'Lord, who has sired winning stock in Australia.

The Santosha kennel owned by Susan and David Crossley based their kennel on Lhakang and Greenmoss strains. Their first champion, made up in 1973, was Ch. Santosha Rambling Rose (by Ch. Chin-Ling of Greenmoss). Then they purchased Tomtru of Lhakang, pale fawn/white who has sired some splendid stock, including black/white Ch. Santosha Bewitched, made up in 1978. He also sired Ch. Khumar China Silk of Darralls (dam of Ch. Darralls Felicity) bred by June Edwards and owned by Dorothy Gurney. In 1979 the Crossleys made up Ch. Santosha Sundown, a brilliant gold/white bitch, sired by Elfann Golden Sunrise of Tricina and in 1981 Ch. Santosha Sunking, a bright gold dog sired by Lhakang Babu of Bodinic. Santosha Nijinski has recently been exported to Mrs. Jean Seddon in South Africa and in 1982 he won the Utility Breed Show in Johannesburg. The Santosha dogs have beautiful heads and colouring.

Ch. Santosha Sunking: Best of Breed Crufts 1984

Another of our older kennels, Snaefell, owned by Audrey Dadds, has been very successful recently. Her original stock derived from Lady Brownrigg's Taishan strain, with some Antarctica line. Of recent years the driving force has been Ch. Newroots Nanki Poo of Snaefell, a son of Ch. Greenmoss Chinki of Meo. Ch. Buttons of Snaefell, sired by Ch. Zeus of Bridgend (himself descended from Chinki) gained his title in 1980. Buttons sired Snaefell Charm, a well known winner. Mrs. Dadds is not too interested in exporting, although in earlier days Gwen Teele in Australia obtained Hia Nan of Snaefell from her. Recently Snaefell Tomsk and Snaefell Raffles have been exported to Sweden and Snaefell Sunshine to South Africa where all three have won their titles.

Mrs. Eunice Fox's 'Whitethroat' kennel (founded on Lhakang and Elfann lines) is inactive at the present due to ill health. In the past Eunice has produced some beautiful dogs in black/white and gold/white. Her well known dog Ch. Jen-kai-ko of Lhakang was Best of Breed, Crufts 1970. His forebears descend from the 'Lunghwa' line, one of the last to come from China, so that he did much to establish this good black/white strain. The colour was in danger of being swamped by the fashion for gold and fawn shades. Eunice bred three Champions, black/white Whitethroat Chinese Gem, gold/white Whitethroat Little Missee (both small, high quality bitches) and the dog Whitethroat Suna of Berinshill, gold-brown/white, owned by Ms. Waugh and Boyle.

Mrs. Widdrington's Lhakang kennel carries on in a small way with descendents of her black/white and gold and fawn lines. Lhakang Cassius, fawn/black mask, has been campaigned successfully to his Junior Warrent by Yvonne Brooker.

A new breed club was formed in 1982 - the Shih Tzu Club of Scotland to provide for people living north of the border where there are a number of successful kennels. Jim Peat's 'Kareth' kennel made up their first champion, Kareth Krishna in 1975 - a daughter of Ch. Greenmoss Chinki of Meo and granddaughter of Ch. Jen-kai-ko of Lhakang. The solid gold bitch Kareth Khoir Angel was made up at Crufts 1982 and was sired by solid apricot Lhakang Babu of Bodinic. Jim also bred Mrs. Young's black/white Ch. Kareth Kestral of Ritoung, who gained his title in 1980. He is a grandson of Ch. Tricina Haku and also carried Lhakang, Whitethroat and Greenmoss breeding.

Jim and Vicki Grugan started their 'Jardhu' kennels from Greenmoss foundations. Their bright gold/white dog Ch. Jardhu Wuffles Wu being a son of Ch. Greenmoss Glory Bee. For the short time they have been in the breed they have done remarkably well and bred some nice bitches.

Bert Easden and Philip Martin have one champion to their credit, Ch. Yankee Chang Yeh, a bright gold/white bitch made up in 1981 and sired by Australian Ch. Greenmoss Geronimo ex. a Keytor bitch. Yankee Yu-tang has won two Championships to date.

Mr. and Mrs. Harvie have had long association with the breed through Mrs. Harvie's mother, Mrs. Inglis (owner of Mr. Wu of Lhakang). They have bred some nice offspring from their bitch Santosha Moonglow by Ch. Greenmoss Glory Bee and Yankee Yu-tang (belonging to Easden and Martin) and have acquired an attractive pale gold/white dog from Terry Morgan, Mort of Bellakerne who is making his mark in the show ring. He is by Ch. Greenmoss Chinki's Fling.

There has been keen interest in the breed for many years in Ireland and recently there have been some good imports from England. Mr. Turkington now owns Ch. Lingchee Jay Tung, a black/white dog of Telota/Antarctica lines, bred by Mrs. Ling who was disbanding her kennels. The English Kennel Club allocated Challenge Certificates for the breed for the first time at Belfast Ch. Show in 1980, which was an inducement for English exhibitors to make the journey and provide stronger competition. That year Shih Tzus drew the largest entry in the Utility Group. The Irish Kennel Club offer Green stars for the breed in Eire. The Shih Tzu Club of Ireland have an excellent secretary and enthusiastic committee who have the interest of the breed at heart. Pearl Reynolds, a Shih Tzu enthusiast for many years, owned the first Shih Tzu to be made up in Ireland - Irish Ch. Hollybrough Hwa of Telota, who died in 1976 at the age of fourteen. Her Chenresi Khasmar gained his title in 1973 when still a puppy.

Recent Irish Champions are:-

1981

- o Jon Jo of Nosredna (male) owned by Mr. W. Turkington
- o Royal Kimbo of Niwanki (male) owned by Mrs. Hilary Walsh (Ballyfrema/Telota)
- o Aisling Cheeki Charlie (male) owned by Mrs. Jane Keene (Greenmoss/Taonan)
- o Bellebanes Pastaza (male) owned by Mr. Frankie McDaid (Crowvalley)

1982

- o Suwanki Lady Love (bitch) owned by Mrs. D. King (Greenmoss/Taonan)
- o Mai of Derdea (bitch) owned by Mrs. D. King (Greenmoss/Taonan)

This chapter would not be complete without mentioning those breeders who may only own a few dogs and have not the opportunity to attend many shows, but despite this, have made up one of their dogs to be a Champion.

- Mrs. Stephenson's Ch. Jaivonne Glimmer of Hope (Greenmoss on both sides).
- Mrs. Ellis' Ch. Fernell Spring Bandit (a Ch. Dominic of Telota G-son) and his son (made up in 1982) Ch. G-Fernell Mista Magic.
- Mrs. Devine's Ch. Kadwen Yan Tsi (grandson of Ch. Jen-kai-ko of Lhakang and Ch. Greenmoss Chinki of Meo).
- Miss Wray's Ch. Meriadoc Kehedin (by Ch. Dominic of Telota).
- Ms. Carey and Coulson's Ch. Fishponds Soo Sze (grandson of Ch. Newroots Nankie Poo of Snaefell).
- Marjorie Kaye's Ch. Bowstones Meena of Attocyl (Greenmoss/Antarctica lines).
- Mrs. Gardiner's Ch. Eastelms Teo Chi (grandson of Ch. Dominic of Telota).
- John Heath's Ch. Hiona Babee of Cijena (by Ch. Bellakerne Zippity-Do).
- Pauline Brook's Ch. Elanzo Chao of Sarosim (Elanzo and Elfann lines).
- Mrs. L. Johnson's Ch. Keltina Ssu Shih wen Shu (by Crowvalley Mandarin).
- Valerie Goodwin's Ch. Queensfield Tutsi Wong (a complete outcross from above).
- Mr. & Mrs. R. Lewis' Ch. Shirwen Han Sum Bee (dam Susie Bee of Greenmoss).
- Mr. & Mrs. P. Jackson's Paora Suki Shoo of Chaulin (bred by Mr. Draper).

The pedigree of the above dogs shows that they all come from a few prepotent sires and dams which bodes well for consistency of type in the future.

There are many dogs besides famous show winners who have never come near the ring, or never been campaigned seriously for one reason or another, yet have made a lasting contribution to the breed. Showing involves time, expense, handling ability and the right kind of general know-how, also a dog that likes to show itself off. The number of prizes a good dog can win will depend on the number of shows its owners can attend, whilst equally good dogs may not have this opportunity.

Some people prefer the breeding side or are pet owners who breed an occasional well thought out litter. It is important to remember such dogs and their owners in this study and the service they have given to the breed. A perusal of pedigrees will reveal repeating names of dogs and bitches who have been veritable pillars of the breed.

Here is a brief list of *some of the* contributors:

o   Many of Audrey Fowler's Chasmu dogs, mostly solid gold or gold/white including red/gold Li Ti Po of Chasmu. d.

o   Lhakang Mimosa of Northallerton (bred by Mrs. Backhouse) who linked with the Chasmus to produce a long line of solid gold.

o   Jungfultets Jung-Ming d. (owned by Mrs. Longden) 1959 Swedish import who brought in an important fresh bloodline which was used universally.

o Tackla Sahib of Lhakang, d. who descended from an important new line from the Far East.

o Elfann Maya Wen of Ricksoo (dam of Ch. Greenmoss Chinki of Meo).

o Cindy-tu of Ricksoo, litter sister to above, who founded a strong line both in solid golds and oartis. Both the above were solid black.

o Many 'Lhakangs' that were put out on breeding terms whilst new lines from abroad were being incorporated.

o Golden Bobbin of Elfann (dam of Int. Ch. Golden Peregrine of Elfann and numerous other winners at home and abroad).

o Hyning Yessir, withdrawn from the ring because of an eye injury.

Amongst others who have been the foundation of important lines are:-

Susanah of Antarctica	Miss Bridge's 'Sampa' dogs
Ching-yo of Elfann	Holmvallee Lao-Yeh of Lhakang
Brownhills Yu Honey	Sing-hi of Lhakang
Brownhills Terasa of Elfann	Tricina Kylin
Hsiang Shieh of Liddesdale	Corwvalley Yameeto
Marnie of Myarlune	Wyesarge Jade Lotus Bud

Everyone who owns beautiful dogs today owes a big thank you to all those, who from earliest times, strove to strengthen and improve the breed, often with limited stock at the start, and later to incorporate untried bloodlines from the Far East and other countries. This is a labour of love for it can take several generations to stabilise type again after an outcross. So don't let's be too complacent about our own success; a lot of it is due to the endless endeavour of those who have gone before, plus some good judgement and a little bit of luck along the way.

CHAPTER 17

THE SHIH TZU ARRIVES IN WESTERN EUROPE

THE SHIH TZU IN THE FAR EAST AND FIRST IMPORTS

The full story of the first Shih Tzus to arrive on the Continent of Europe is told in the chapter on Scandinavia, but it is necessary to regress a little to see how these dogs became the foundation stock in other European countries.

In 1932 Mme. Henrik Kauffmann, wife of the Danish Minister in China, introduced the first three specimens into Scandinavia when Herr Kauffmann was transferred to Norway from Pekin. Mme. Kauffmann first came across these dogs in a dramatic way in the early 1930's, when she begged for the lives of several about to be burnt to death in a ceremony (probably connected with a funeral rite). She managed to take one of these dogs for herself - a black/white bitch named Schauder, and was so enchanted by her character that she decided to find two more. After a search of eighteen months, when she discarded scores of large coarse dogs, she finally found a small-type black/white male, Aidzo, and lastly she had the great good fortune to obtain a golden bitch, Leidza, from one of the Eunuchs from the Imperial Palace, born in 1928.

This was just three years after the young Emperor had been expelled from the Palace and had taken refuge with the Japanese in Tientsin, and she was the last known Shih Tzu to come from the Palace. Mme. Kauffmann considered her to be a very beautiful specimen - better than Schauder who was high on the leg. In each case only the sire and dam of these three dogs was known by name.

These dogs were first registered as "Lhasa Terriers", one of the names they had been known by in China. In 1934 the breed was recognised under the name of "Shih Tzu" by the *Fédération Cynologique Internationale*, the central association to which national dog clubs in Europe are affiliated, and the F.C.I. adopted and promulgated the standard approved by the English Kennel Club the same year. However, the name remained "Lhasa Terrier" in Norway itself until 1939, and was only changed after correspondence between the Norsk Kennel Club and Lady Brownrigg in England.

It is interesting to note that Mme. Kauffmann's three original imports to Norway had scissor-bite <u>overshot</u> mouths, which she described as "level", i.e. "the lower teeth fitting in behind the upper ones", and this remained in the Scandinavian standard until 1974, when it was changed to "level or slightly <u>undershot</u>" in keeping with the British standard.

In 1933 Queen Maud of Norway, brought one of the Kauffmann's puppies, Choo-Choo, (a black/white son of Aidzo and Schauder) to England and presented him to the Duchess of York, (later the Queen Mother). He proved very fashionable at stud and his line was perpetuated in British stock.

It is sad that none of the dogs belonging to Mme. Graeffe, wife of the Belgian Ambassador in Pekin, continued in European stock, although one of them, a dog named "Mei-yun" won a first prize at the *Exposition Canine de Paris* in 1929, when the Graeffes were home on leave. It was thanks to them and other eminent European diplomats, who were in China at the very end of the Dynastic system, that some of the Palace dogs were preserved. The Graeffes had heard about the Tibetan dogs sent as "tribute" to the Chinese Court by the 13th Dalai Lama and predecessors, and were most anxious to track them down. When the Empress Tzu-Hsi had to flee after the Boxer rebellion in

1900, she gave orders to the Palace officials that most of her dogs were to be destroyed so that they would not fall into alien hands, but a few were smuggled out of the Palace for breeding purposes. She returned to the Capital in 1902, and received the last specimens from Tibet in 1908, shortly before her death; a few specimens were known to exist in the Palace up till the late 1920's although the young puppet Emperor, Pu Yi, had sacked all the Eunuchs (who cared for the dogs) by 1923, and it is said that their breeding languished sadly.

Due to the influence M. Graeffe had with the Prime Minister, some of the Shih Tzu-type dogs were traced to the Interior, where they had been taken earlier by the Eunuchs for safe custody; members of the French and Italian Legations managed to obtain specimens, and the Graeffes obtained their original pair, "Lize" and "Kwanine", from a predecessor at the Belgian Embassy. They managed to obtain another from the Italian Legation - all from Palace stock. These dogs were said to be "brown and golden" - presumably gold/brindle. Mme. Graeffe held the opinion that the parti-colour dogs were produced by crossing with the Japanese Spaniel. Usually the Chinese were very loath to let these dogs fall into the hands of "foreign devils", and sometimes gave them powdered glass in their food so that they would not survive the journey to foreign parts.

The whole story has to be seen against a backcloth of troubled times in China; first the Boxer rebellion, the death of the old Empress, then the collapse of the Dynastic system four years later. In 1933, on a rise of nationalism, the Japanese invaded Manchuria and by 1937, after bombing Shanghai and Canton, the invasion was complete and foreigners living in China went through difficult and uncertain times. In 1941, the Japanese entered World War II against the Western Allies with the U.S.A. finally surrendering and being forced to withdraw from China after the Americans dropped atomic bombs on Hiroshima and Nagasaki. It was then the turn of Chairman Mao's Communist Armies to sweep across China with a final takeover in 1949 by which time most of the foreigners had left. By Mao's orders all pet dogs had to be destroyed and any found wandering the streets were stoned to death, which was the end of the Shih Tzu or Apso type in mainland China. The lucky ones were brought out with military and diplomatic personnel to countries in Europe and the New World. A black/white Shih Tzu, almost killed by stoning, was rescued by an English woman nursed back to health and returned to England with her. It was only his strong constitution which saved his life.

The Graeffes were devoted Shih Tzu owners, and refused to be parted from them, so that the dogs travelled with them from China to France, back to Persia, then to Switzerland and finally settled with their owners in Holland. When the Graeffes were transferred to Teheran, Persia, in the late 1930's they took six specimens with them - descendents of Lize and Kwanine, the original pair from Palace stock obtained in the previous decade. On their pedigree these dogs were called "Lhasa Lion-dog" or Apso from the "Palais Imperial, Pekin". The word "Apso" was considered to be merely a descriptive term given to any small, shaggy dog, meaning "Goat-like". This pedigree shows that a descendent of Lize and Kwanine, a male named "Foshin", won a second prize at the Pekin Kennel Club Show in 1934. It is very likely that Lize and Kwanine were related quite closely to "Leidza" also from the Palace, but the former two would be an earlier generation.

It would be so interesting if the parchment scrolls, on which the most beautiful of the Palace dogs of this period were depicted, ever came to light, but doubtless the Communists destroyed valuable records of this kind during the Cultural Revolution, especially as they did not like pet dogs - only the edible or herding kind.

Lize and Kwanine had their first litter in Pekin in 1927, and a son from this liaison, Mei-yun, mentioned previously, sired a litter in

Paris in 1935 to a bitch named Lung-lin from the same ancestry, producing five puppies. Mei-yun died in Paris in 1936, but Lung-lin travelled out East again with the Graeffes when they were posted to Teheran. Here Lung-lin produced another litter in 1937 by Foshin. They were prevailed upon to present a bitch puppy to Fawzia, the Persian Empress, thus becoming inaccessible for breeding. They retained the only other bitch, but unfortunately it died of distemper, and so were only left with males.

When the Graeffes met Mrs Sheila Bode (later a well known English breeder and judge) in Teheran, and found that she had brought out a Pekingese bitch with her from England, they decided to use one of their dogs, "Tao-tie" on this bitch with Mrs. Bode's consent. They explained to her that cross-breeding had been resorted to by the Chinese Empress Tzu-Hsi in order to reduce the size of the Tibetan dogs and develop the shorter, slightly bowed front legs and flatter face which the Empress admired. So Princess Chu-tzu, an orange Pekingese, was bred to Tao-tie resulting in four male puppies born in 1940, all of which finished cream coloured with black tips to their ear-fringes.

Mrs. Bode writes:

All these puppies resembled their sire rather than the Peke, having profuse coats, beards and whiskers, sturdy bodies, short faces and legs. They were all fairly small, similar in size to the Graeffes Palace stock, being in the 10-12 lbs. range, with the exception of Kai-tzu (Kai-kai as I called him) who was smaller with a flatter face, more in the 8 - 9 lbs. range. One puppy, Wang-ti, died of pneumonia soon after birth, having crawled out of his box at night, but I kept the other three. Unfortunately one of these - Tao-tzu was run over by a car and had to be put to sleep. They all had good jaw formation.

I was desperate at leaving them behind (especially my special pet, Kai-kai) when we returned to England at short notice in 1944 as my husband, Kenneth, needed emergency hospital treatment. However the Graeffes came to the rescue and took my dogs. Kai-kai pined terribly, but in the end settled happily with a French friend of the Graeffes, returned to Paris with her after the war, and died at about eight years of age. Chiang-tzu, the other dog, became very bossy with the Graeffes other dogs, so went as a companion to Mme. Graeffe's mother and died in Switzerland aged twelve". A litter-brother of Tao-tie's, named "Lao-ho" was presented by the Graeffes to the Queen of the Belgians.

It is worth diverging here to recount how Sheila and Ken Bode first became acquainted with this type of dog. They travelled extensively in the Middle and Far East for over twenty years, in connection with Ken's work. One day they were given a little dog, very small and golden-brown in colour whilst in Tabriz, Northern Persia. He had a profuse coat with hair over the eyes and tea-pot handle tail. They had no idea what breed he represented, being unacquainted with the Palace dogs at the time, but he was a very quaint and charming little creature. He had only been in their possession for three weeks when he was stolen - during the afternoon siesta he had wandered out into the garden and was never seen again - probably stolen by one of the servants for their womenfolk. As all women at that time lived in purdah, it was impossible to find him again.

In 1935 they found a second one, looking exactly the same as the first, who was presented to Ken by a tanker driver who had picked his up in Kurdistan. After about a month, he too was stolen whilst they were living in an Oil Refinery outside Kermanshah on the Persian Gulf. He was smuggled into the town, probably by one of the coolies when he went into the Bazaar for their daily shopping. Their cook reported having seen him in the town being chased and stoned by boys. The Bodes managed to track him down, but he was completely dazed and with severe head injuries, obviously due to stoning, and had to be put to sleep. These little dogs attracted a lot of attention from the Persians as they were so quaint and unusual, which is probably why they were stolen, very likely from their European owners. When Ken and Sheila Bode moved to Teheran in 1939 they became acquainted with M. and Mme. Graeffe, and were delighted when it was discovered that they owned a similar kind of dog and were able to throw light on their origin and history. By this time the Graeffes' dogs appeared to have faded in colour from the golden shades favoured in the Palace, as Mrs. Bode recalls that they were mostly white with grey furnishings.

Writing to Sheila Bode from The Hague in 1947, where they had finally come to rest, Mme. Graeffe said that she considered the Shih Tzu to be the most interesting type of dog she had ever owned. At that time she still had three of them - Tahoudze (Whiskers), son of Lize, who had been born in Pekin in 1931, in beautiful coat and enjoying his food and walks - he died the following year at the great age of seventeen.

She also owned his daughter, Pouseli, born in Teheran in 1937, and grandson, Marqui, then aged seven. Shortly after this, whilst driving in the Hague, Mme. Graeffe was involved in a terrible motor accident from which she lost much of her vitality, only recovering very slowly and suffering from paralysis of the eyes and voice for many months. After her husband's death she moved to Palma Nova, Majorca, where she lived a very secluded life, and no more is heard of her valuable strain of dogs.

The Comtesse René d'Anjou, a French aristocrat living in Pekin, owned a large kennel of Shih Tzus and started breeding in 1935. She was a friend of the Princess Der-ling, who had for two years been

Lady-in-Waiting to the Old Empress Tzu-Hsi in the Forbidden City, and had written several books about Palace life. When they met in 1935, the Princess was able to give the Comtesse first-hand accounts of the Royal Kennels.

The Comtesse explained the difficulty she had in finding good specimens to found the kennel in Pekin. The Chinese had been selling her their worst specimens which grew up to be too long in the leg or nose, and had either reverted to ancestral type or been cross-bred. After that she had to make it a rule to buy only adult dogs of the honey or pure golden colour, and under twelve pounds in weight, as favoured in the Palace.

In 1946 the Comte and Comtesse d'Anjou left China and settled in Juan-le-Pins, France, but they did not bring any of their dogs back with them. Writing to the Misses Wild in England (Cotsvale Shih Tzu and Apso kennels) in 1950 we learn that

> *Comtesse Rene d'Anjou bred Shih Tzus for many years in Pekin, winning highest honours at the shows there. At least four of her puppies were sent to new owners in Europe before the War, but as all her papers had to be abandoned in Pekin, she cannot remember the names of the purchasers.*
>
> *During the Japanese occupation, owing to the great scarcity of food etc., her lovely dogs had to be put down.*
>
> *The Comtesse is now settled in France at Juan-le-Pins and it is her ambition to start breeding again. She is only interested in the honey-coloured or honey-and white variety, and the small type.*

In 1940, whilst still in Pekin, she gave a puppy to the wife of the U.S. Naval Attaché, who by strange coincidence has just arrived in Beaulieu-sur-Mer with the original male, now ten years old, and his five year old son. The Comtesse is hoping to obtain a bitch to mate to the young dog.

The Comtesse believed that these dogs were pure in origin and had remained so for nearly 300 years, since the first specimens were presented to K'an-hsi, famous first Emperor of the Manchu (Ch'ing) Dynasty in 1643. This makes a romantic story but is somewhat fanciful and contrary to accounts written by historians who claim that the Shih Tzu became distinct from the Apso through judicious crossing with the Imperial Pekingese in the Palace. It is unrealistic to assume absolute purity or great antiquity for any breed of dog in a situation where no records were kept and type was distinctly variable.

The d'Anjous co-operated with other fanciers to produce a standard for the breed in France - " Chien-Lion de Tibet" (Lion-dogs of Tibet) as they were called at that period. The Comte had been President of the Pekin Kennel Club, formed in 1934, and instrumental in drawing up a standard there under the name of "Lhasa Lion-dog" with the help of Mme de Breuil, a Russian refugee. This standard was based on a book written by Mme. Lu Zee Yuen Nee, a Chinese woman who owned a kennel of about 30 of these dogs in Pekin in the 1930's and exhibited successfully at the Pekin Kennel Club shows.

This very descriptive booklet with allegorical sketches depicting the points was printed by Imprimrie Na Che Pac, little backstreet people in the Bazaar. Aspects of the original French standard were based on Mme. Lu's book, though most of it was taken from the English standard drawn up in 1934, with minor additions and exceptions.

The Comtesse, writing from Juan-le-Pins in 1935, says:

My husband has made out the characteristics and standard of the 'Shih Tze' (as she called them), as one was non-existent in France - this at the request of various judges who have never seen these dogs before, and who will have them approved by the "Societé Centrale Canine de France".

The following declaration is written at the end of the French standard:

This standard, established in detail by Comte and Comtesse d'Anjou who have reared these dogs in Pekin for many years, has been entirely approved by H.E. Mme. Wilden, owner during a long stay in China of numerous dogs of this breed of a white variety which unfortunately, because of the war, left no descendants. This standard has also received the complete approval of H.E.M. Chayat, Ambassador of France and Paraguay, who, as well as Mme. Wilden, has spent many years in China, having owned large numbers of specimens. M. Chayat judged these dogs at the Pekin Dog Shows.

THE ORIGINAL FRENCH STANDARD

Chien-Lion du Tibet

Characteristics: These are very heavily-coated dogs, with a distinctly arrogant carriage, very active and lively, full of independence and courage. They are very affectionate and have a lot of personality. They are brave, but do not search for trouble. They take correction without batting an eyelid (*sans sourciller*) as if they do not understand why they are being punished. They have the habit of sleeping on their tummies with the paws stretched out before and behind, so that it is difficult to distinguish head from tail, the coat being thick and abundant.

Head:	Large and round, shock-headed with the hair falling over the eyes; good beard and whiskers, giving the head a chrysanthemum-like appearance.
Eyes:	Well-spaced, large, round and dark, and hidden by the hair.
Muzzle:	Square and short, flat and hairy, but not wrinkled like a Pekingese.
Ears:	Large and drooping and so abundantly coated that they blend with the hair of the neck.
Mouth:	Level or slightly undershot. *An overshot jaw is a serious fault.*
Body:	Length from withers to root of tail - considerably longer than height at withers; well-ribbed up; *lower in front than behind. The opposite is a serious fault.*
Legs:	Short, muscular and straight, very hairy, thighs muscular.
Feet:	Large and well-padded with hair between the toes. They should look big on account of the wealth of hair.

Tail: Should be well-plumed and carried gaily over the back.

Coat: Should have a woolly undercoat, and topcoat long, fine and silky, non-wavy, and falling to the ground in the most beautiful specimens.

Neck: Short and strong.

Chest: Spacious.

Apron and Breeches: Well-furnished and long, making the most typical feature in the silhouette of these dogs.

Colour: All colours permissible, solid and parti-colour. In the black and white, a white flash on the forehead and a white tip to the tail are much appreciated. Chestnut coloured dogs can have nose of the same colour and lighter eyes. Honey coloured and white are rare and much appreciated.

Dimensions: Height at withers approximately 23 - 26 cm. (9 - 10¼ ins.)

Weight: 3 - 10 kilos (11 - 22 lbs.)
Preference: 5 - 7 kilos (11 - 15½ lbs.)

Scale of Points: General appearance 20,
Head 15,
Balance 20,
Coat 20,
Tail 15.

The History of the Shih Tzu

In correspondence between Mrs. Lenox, Mrs. Widdrington and the Comtesse, the latter said that she considered that the weights set in the French standard were too high, but everyone needed accommodating at that time. She recounted how, at the Pekin Kennel Club Shows the question of variation in size was overcome by dividing into two sizes - "up to and over 12 lbs." which were judged separately. Some of the Shih Tzu in China had been bred down from a much larger dog, possibly the Tibetan Terrier, and reverted easily to it, whilst the Palace dogs were bred small to please the Empress and Ladies of the Court. It is perhaps due to her influence in the past that some of the French dogs are amongst the smallest in the world today.

The Comtesse imported several dogs from England after she settled in France. These were obtained from Mrs. Audrey Fowler's "Chasmu" kennel, who specialised in the golden colours, and flew to Nice with two bitches in 1951 - Golden Chin-to and Golden Yetti, and the following year another bitch, Fe Shaing, and a dog, Golden Fi-lock, were obtained from Mrs Fowler through the intermediary of Col. J.B. Stubbs. Fi-lock became an Italian and International Champion, and his daughter won a CACIB in Monte Carlo. The Comtesse considered it significant that both these dogs had four dew-claws, as the Chinese thought that this meant a perfect dog! The only previous one that she had owned with four dew-claws had become a Champion in Pekin. A son and daughter of Golden Fi-lock and Fe Shaing were exported to U.S.A. in 1953, but there is no evidence that their line continued. At that time a Mme. Dupont owned a prize winning Shih Tzu in Paris of unknown background.

Mrs. Fowler had met the Comtesse d'Anjou whilst on a visit to China in 1936/37, and took back to England two bitches, one "Nui-san", bred by the Comtesse and the other, "Fu-tzu" bred by Miss Bieber, an expert on the "Lion-dog Legend". Unfortunately these dogs were never bred, and died during World War II, so that none of the

98

Comtesse's Chinese strain continued in the Western World.

The Comtesse did not think that there were any "pure-bred" Tibetan Shih Tzus left in Pekin when she left that city in 1946. In 1949 the Peoples' Republic of China put a ban on all pet dogs and they had to be destroyed, as previously stated. Catherine d'Anjou died in her daughter's home in Canada in 1965, and the world was poorer for the loss of this elegant lady with her wide knowledge and interest in the Tibetan Lion-dog.

Mrs. Doreen Lenox was an Englishwoman who brought some of her dogs back to Europe with her when she had to flee China. She had owned a small kennel of "Tibetans" as she called them, when her husband was Manager of a Bank in Shanghai in the 1940's and 50's. She obtained a striking dog, Dandy of Shanghai, from a Chinese couple. He was solid red-gold with coat to the ground. The Chinese owners knew nothing about the background of his parents, who were also very beautiful dogs - the sire pure white, and the dam clear golden.

When some friends, Commander and Mrs. James Madison Doyle, arrived in Shanghai from Annapolis, they brought with them a clear fawn bitch, "Chu-Chu", who was registered with the American Kennel Club as Hamilton Maru and put on the Lhasa Apso register, (at a time when no distinction was made between Shih Tzus and Apsos in U.S.A.). She was left with Mrs. Lenox to be mated to Dandy when her owners had to go away. "Chu-Chu" produced four puppies in 1946, and Mrs. Lenox kept an apricot bitch, "Hsing-erth" whilst another bitch, "Ishuh Tzu" eventually went to General Alex Telfer-Smollet on the shores of Loch Lomond in Scotland, after a perilous journey home from China. This attractive young bitch was "small, gay and fearless" - none the worse for the long journey home and the six month's quarantine in England. Ishuh Tzu was registered as a Shih Tzu and mated to one of the General's home-bred dogs - black and white "Wu", in 1948 founding a line in which the solid colours of her ancestors - blacks, gold and honey shades, came through strongly. As Mrs. Fowler was interested in these shades, she used the descendants of Ishuh Tzu to establish them, particularly the golden colour in her Chasmu kennel, and in later years Ishuh Tzu's progeny crossed the English Channel to various countries on the Continent of Europe.

Many of Mrs Lenox's Tibetans were in fact more the Lhasa Apso type, at a time when the distinctions between the two breeds were not yet understood in some countries; however the selected descendants of Ishuh Tzu were satisfactorily established in British and European Shih Tzus through her handsome black son Shebo Schunde of Hungjao, and her black daughter, Yram Chingling of Hungjao; the outcross brought in much needed new blood and virility after the war years.

Mrs. Lenox and her husband had to put up with some very trying experiences in Shanghai due to the political situation in China. They returned to Europe in the early 1950's after a period in Hong-Kong; here the dogs were quarantined and registered with the Hong-Kong Kennel Club under the kennel name of "Chapoo". Whilst they were settling in France, General Telfer-Smollett housed several of the bitches, but finally Hsing-ern (apricot) and daughter, Hung-mei (silver-fox) sired by P'u-chi, a dog owned by Mrs. Price in Shanghai, rejoined the family in France. Hsing-ern's dam, Chu-chu, had died in 1951, but Dandy and his son, Chientang, were also able to rejoin their owners again in France, living in Vence for some years and then settling in Malaga, Spain. In 1978, Mrs. Lenox acquired a solid red/gold bitch Ching-yu of Lhakang (Mitzi) from Mrs. Widdrington, a descendant of Ishuh Tzu, as a mate for her own remaining dog, then eleven years old, but they never produced any offspring, although her line proliferated in the British Isles. Mitzi went to Switzerland with her mistress in the hot weather, where she revelled in the mountain air.

THE SHIH TZU ARRIVES IN WESTERN EUROPE

One of Ishuh Tzu's sons, Shebo Schunde of Hungjao went to Denmark from England in 1951 to the kennel of Fru Hansa Anderson, and brought in fresh blood to the Scandinavian strain which had been continually inbred since their arrival in Norway twenty years earlier. Although he was a very big dog, his line spread in European countries, and continued in exports to U.S.A., including in stock imported by Mrs. Ingrid Colwell.

EARLY EUROPEAN KENNELS

The foundation stock of European kennels which continue today came from Scandinavian countries and from the British Isles. Later on Shih Tzus were also imported from Australia and the United States.

The main pioneers of the breed in European countries were three ladies - in Denmark, Frøken Astrid Jeppesen and her mother, Frau Erika Geusendam in West Germany, and Mejuffrouw Eta Pauptit in Holland.

Frøken Jeppesen founded her "Bjorneholms" kennel in 1947 with stock descended from Aidzo, Leidza and Schauder, the three first imports which were brought to Norway from China in 1932 by the Danish diplomat Herr Henrik Kauffmann and his wife. Frøken Jeppesen purchased her foundation bitch, Mai-ling av Dux, from Mr. John Norman of Oslo, which descended from the Kauffmann's dogs. Her dog, Bjorneholms Lyemun and her bitch Bjorneholms Kotzu, were second generation from Aidzo and Leidza, and her dog, Bjorneholms Kesang was third generation. This kennel has produced thirty Champions and exported numerous Shih Tzus to other European countries, including Scandinavia and also the United States. Denmark has a very important position in the European Shih Tzu world as many breeders started with dogs from the old Scandinavian lines, particularly from the Bjorneholms kennel and, although these lines have been inbred for over half century, their owners claim few serious genetic problems. The original small type, as bred in the Imperial Palace, Pekin, is carefully cultivated to this day and a little English or Dutch blood has been added to improve body and bone and to keep them low on the leg.

In 1955 Mrs. Erne Jungefeldt introduced her first Shih Tzu, a bitch named Bjorneholms Pippi, into her famous kennel of Airedales. Both parents of Jungfultets Jung-Ming, exported to England in 1959, were from the Bjorneholms kennel. This was in the significant exchange with the black and white English dog, Fu-ling of Clystvale, bred by Mrs. Meg Longden, who introduced much needed new blood into the Scandinavian lines; a small heavy dog, he was a prepotent sire and produced many Champion offspring and became one himself. He was sixth generation from a Peking outcross introduced into English stock in 1952 to improve type.

Frøken Jeppesen continued breeding until 1977; her niece Frøken Merete Kjaer has some of her aunt's stock and is continuing her line and hopes to inherit her kennel name.

Miss Kjaer's dogs descend from the original Scandinavian lines, plus the Australian "Geltree" line, and from the special "Lhakang" litter bred for Frau Geusendam in 1971. None of these lines contain the Pekingese outcross carried out in England in 1952. Her late stud dog, D.K. Chandra v. Tschomo-Lungma, a sturdy 13 lb. dog, who became a Champion at the age of ten years, was sired by Hsieng-Feng of Lhakang out of Lakshmi v. Tschomo-Lungma and has produced some good puppies. Miss Kjaer is a lover of the small Shih Tzu and her aim is to keep size down whilst maintaining strong bone and sturdy bodies.

Frau Geusendam obtained stock for her "Tschomo-Lungma"

kennel from Frøken Jeppesen in 1969, and they worked in partnership for many years, facilitated by the fact that Frau Geusendam lives in Lübeck in Northern Germany, not far from the Danish border. Her most successful dog was Int. Ch. Ollo vom Tschomo-Lungma, by Bjorneholms Pif out of Bjorneholms Ting-a-ling. This bitch was also the dam of the Champion bitches Tangra and Tang-la v. Tschomo-Lungma, sired by Bjorneholms Bhadro. Int. Ch. Naga v. Tschomo-Lungma is the dam of six International Champions. By 1984 Frau Geusendam had bred twenty-two International Champions and had made up five more herself. She had won the Shih Tzu title at the F.C.I. Annual World Championship Show on ten occasions, eight of them with home-bred dogs. Shih Tzus bred by her have won titles in fourteen countries.

Mejuffrouw Eta Pauptit's first breed were Afghan hounds, which she started to breed in the mid-thirties, when the first Afghans were introduced to Holland. She took her kennel name "Oranje Manege" from her father's riding school. She herself was an accomplished horsewoman and used to exercise her Afghans and Salukis on horseback. The Oranje Manege Afghans became famous and remained so for many years. In 1962 Mej. Pauptit decided to take up a smaller breed, and after careful consideration she chose the Shih Tzu. Her foundation bitch, Pi-tze, was the daughter of Ch. Fu-ling of Clystvale (the English stud dog imported into Sweden in 1959) out of Jungfultets Jung Wu Pi. Pi-Tze's first litter by a Swedish dog - Bedlams Kanshung Ling - in 1962, produced Hang Shu v.d. Oranje Manege who became an International Champion. Many more were to follow, making her Shih Tzus famous, both in Holland and overseas. Mej. Pauptit continued breeding with great influence on the development of the Shih Tzu in Europe until 1977.

The first Shih Tzu litter had been bred in Holland in 1962 by Mej. Backx-Bennick's "Reeuwyks" kennel with English stock from

Antarctica and Chasmu kennels, also a dog from West Germany. Dogs of English and Scandinavian origins were bred together and the two types began to merge.

The late Baroness Beatrice van Ponthaleon van Eck combined these lines with Tschomo-Lungma and Oranje Manege stock in her "Blauwe Mammoth" kennel. Sadly, she was killed in a car crash, but her kennel was continued by younger members of her family. Mej. Renzing, "Kleine Oosterling" kennel, and Mijnheer v.d. Spek, "Klein Vossenburg" kennel, also contributed to the build-up of Shih Tzus in Holland.

During the sixties the number of Shih Tzus in Western Europe slowly increased; the dogs were of two distinct types - those of the Scandinavian line were small and slender, usually pale gold, pastel or red-brown with black masks, and with gentle affectionate natures. Those imported from the British Isles were generally parti-colour, more sturdily built, larger and more independent in character. British dogs carried their tails in an arch, according to their standard, balancing the head, whereas the Scandinavian tail was laid lower on the back or in a screw.

Although a slightly undershot mouth was permitted in the standard which the F.C.I. had promulgated (which was based on the English Kennel Club standard), West Europeans preferred a level bite, although it meant a weaker chin. Full dentition was important, even in such a short-nosed breed, and missing incisors or pre-molars were penalised. Most judges preferred straight front legs and this tended to produce a narrower brisket and rib-cage. The broad, deep chest required in the English standard was more likely to produce a slight curve in the upper forearm (which could be felt when the dog was handled) and a rolling gait. This did not often find favour, especially if the top line was not level.

It is interesting to recall that the original French standard, drawn up by the Comte and Comtesse d'Anjou after their return from Pekin in 1946, based on the dogs they and others owned in China, states: "lower in front than behind; the opposite is a serious fault". The Chinese standard, formulated by the Pekin Kennel Club, permitted the front to be "slightly bowed" with the subsequent slope of the top line towards the front - it was important to the Chinese that the Tibetan Lion-Dog should be bred in the image of the "Lion Rampant"! This and other characteristics, such as flared eyes and a double row of lower incisors, cultivated by the Chinese, have often been hard to breed out. One day a lady who had lived in China approached a Shih Tzu owner at a show and asked "Are these the dogs who comb their own hair with the claws on their hind legs?" To this end she assumed that the nails should never be cut, but allowed to grow as long as possible!

Chenmo of Lhakang

There was controversy about the benefits of the Pekingese outcross made in England in 1952, when the breed seemed to be veering away from the standard - too many dogs becoming long-nosed, big and rangy. At this period a well known all round English judge, Miss Enid Nichols, recalling the good early type, wrote in a critique, that "She regretted the big rangy, snouty dogs of which there were too many", and Mr. Leo Wilson, another famous all-round judge, wrote on similar lines.

Mrs. Sheila Bode (Shebo kennel), who had first-hand knowledge of the Graeffe's dogs (which were of Palace stock), pointed out that some judges were ruining the breed by putting up the wrong type, and impressed on the judges and owners alike to give more thought to the origin and history of the breed. The outcross was carried out by Miss E.M. Evans, Elfann kennel, a well-known Pekingese breeder, who felt the cross would correct the trend in the wrong direction.This was carried out under Kennel Club regulations which permitted the fourth generation from the outcross to be registered as "pure-bred".

Neither Frøken Jeppesen nor Frau Geusendam approved of it: Frau Geusendam's choice of kennel name "Tschomo-Lungma", the Tibetan name for Mount Everest, reflects her belief that the Shih Tzu is a Tibetan breed. Neither of these ladies would use Shih Tzus descended from the cross in their breeding programmes. Herr Leo Helbig, a prominent German judge, also disapproved of it and went so far as to describe a Shih Tzu containing Pekingese blood as a "bastard hound"! Mevrouw Schoor-Oskam, the well known Dutch judge, took the opposite view and approved of the Pekingese outcross and the selective breeding programme that had followed it, and said that in her opinion "The English have a genius for breeding animals".

Graf Lazar von Lippa, an experienced specialist judge of the small breeds in many countries over forty years, and Registrar of the Verband Klein Hundzuchter (the Small Breed Club), took the same view as Mev. Schoor-Oskam and also approved of the outcross. He had researched the matter carefully and was co-author with Ina von Voss of "Das Kleinhundbuck", a book about the groupings of small breeds with a common ancestry and the development of miniature forms of various breeds.

In this book he suggests that the Shih Tzu is a Sino-Tibetan breed of mixed origin (i.e. from the Temple Dogs of Tibet, and the Imperial Pekingese of China). "In East Asia", he states, "The frontiers or dividing lines between the different types of small dog had never been clearly defined". The Tibetan dogs presented to Mr. Suydam Cutting, an American world traveller, in 1933 by the 13th Dalai Lama, were clearly the Lhasa Apso type, and these dogs became the foundation stock of his famous Hamilton Farm Kennel of Lhasa Apsos in New Jersey. This was the same Dalai Lama who had presented several Tibetan dogs to the Empress Tzu-Hsi of China in 1908 from the same strain shortly before her death.

Mr. Cutting obtained his last imports, "Le" and "Pema" from the 14th Dalai Lama, which were of the same type. From their picture these dogs had rough coats, longer forefaces than the Shih Tzu and flatter heads falling away behind the eyes. This is an important link which makes it clear that the type of dog originally presented to the Imperial Court of China were of the Lhasa Apso type rather than the cross-breeding to produce the short-faced, short-legged dogs from which come our Shih Tzu. In later years the Shih Tzu type probably travelled back to Tibet with trade or military personnel, as we know from Tibetan refugees that specimens of the shorter-nosed type did exist in Tibet before the Chinese takeover in 1950.

Although the Scandinavian dogs had not increased in size in the same way as some of the British dogs, some were tending to become too light and leggy, perhaps through the influence of one of their ancestors - Schauder, to whom they were repeatedly bred back. Later imports of British stock helped to remedy this.

It is not surprising that the small Asian breeds sometimes throw back to a long-forgotten ancestor since they were interbred down through the centuries, not only in the streets, but in the Palaces as well; the Chinese might well say that any argument about cross-breeding was "much ado about nothing"! In earlier generations of the original Scandinavian line, occasional throwbacks occurred to a smooth-coated Tibetan Spaniel-type (and variations on this theme), which appeared in Scandinavian stock exported both to the British Isles and across the Atlantic. And nowadays we hear of "Prapsos" on the Continent of Europe - Tibetan Spaniels appearing in Lhasa Apso litters. Since 1981 the French Kennel Club had permitted these throwbacks to go on the Tibetan Spaniel register, as it is averred that they breed true to type, the main difference from the Apso being in type of coat. Such variations in type open up an interesting window on the past of the small Asian breed.

According to Frau Geusendam there are still approximately thirty Shih Tzus to be found in European countries descending in an unbroken line from the original three imports to Norway in 1932. Miraculously they have survived this close inbreeding for over 50 years! She owns five of them herself and others are to be found in the U.S.A. and in Canada. Trudy Kerr, "Ta Ya Chai" kennel, Alberta, has stock from Frau Geusendam and plans to carry on this line.

In 1969 the Shih Tzu was recognised in the United States of America and quickly became popular there. Consequently there was a great demand for stock from Europe. The Bjorneholms and Tschomo-Lungma kennels, and also many Dutch breeders exported Shih Tzus in large numbers - puppies, whole litters, young dogs, bitches in whelp and adult dogs already qualified as Champions, were shipped across the Atlantic. As a result, breeders in Western Europe suddenly found themselves short of breeding-stock. It was as though the Shih Tzu tide, which had been steadily rising, had turned and ebbed, leaving the seashore rather bare.

Frau Geusendam and Frøken Jeppesen found themselves in especial difficulty as they had set their faces resolutely against the Pekingese outcross, now widely dispersed throughout the breed, and it was difficult to find a source without it. By this time Mej. Pauptit had come to agree with them and shared their predicament. At Frau Geusendam's request, Mrs. Widdrington arranged the breeding of a special litter in 1971 from her stock by Juan of Lhakang, seven years old, ex. Hwa-yin of Lhakang (Waggin), aged eight, daughter of Gun Yiang of Lunghwa, probably the last two English Shih Tzus of breeding age which did not contain the Pekingese outcross. Hwa-yin, who had really been retired from breeding due to her age, nevertheless took this litter in her stride. It was a nephew-to-aunt mating and produced four dogs and one bitch, all parti-colour. Their parents were descended from two of the last Shih Tzu-type dogs to come out of China in 1948 and 1949 -"Wuffles", camel coloured, and "Mai-ting", black and white. Their line was not introduced into English stock until several years later when Mrs. Widdrington managed to obtain a clear black and white bitch, Gun-Yiang of Lunghwa from Mrs. Rowland Morris, who owned these dogs. Not much was known about their ancestry, in fact Wuffles and Mai-ting had been imported "pedigree unknown", but it was thought that the former may have come from the "Ra-shis" kennel of Mr. Alfred Koehn, a German living in Pekin. (In 1951 Mr. Koehn had to flee from China, and settled in Tokyo, but his dogs were left behind with Europeans, and their fate is not known).

Hwa-yin's whole litter was exported to Frau Geusendam, who retained a black and white bitch, Hsi-la of Lhakang, very much smaller than the males. Hsi-la qualified as an International Champion and was bred from. Two of her progeny, Dhuti and Dolsa v. Tschomo-Lungma became Champions, and she has a promising grandson. The dogs were

109

used at stud by the Bjorneholms, Tschomo-Lungma and Oranje Manege kennels.

Another source of Shih Tzus without the Pekingese outcross still existed in Australia. In 1971 Eta Pauptit obtained a bitch on loan from Geusendam - "Geltree Mao Hseuh" bred by Mrs. Teele, descending from Antarctica and Snaefell stock, which had been imported from England before the outcross was made. This bitch was bred to Ch. Ollo v. Tschomo-Lungma and produced a litter of four puppies for Mej. Pauptit after which she became the property of Astrid Jeppesen. The former also obtained a dog, Geltree Pandit, which Frau Geusendam had imported together with his dam. These Australian imports proved much larger and longer in the back than the refined Scandinavian type. They also brought in the liver colouring, but through a selective breeding programme their line was successfully incorporated.

Elsewhere, European breeders used stock of both British and Scandinavian origin, and two types began to emerge; there was little strong feeling about the Pekingese outcross and most people bred according to appearance rather than background. An English bitch, Wu-ying of Lhakang, sired by Mister Wu of Lhakang out of Old-Gold of Tawnyridge, became an International Champion, whilst her owner, Major Elizabeth Ross, was serving with the British Army in Germany from 1965 to 1968. She was eighth generation from the outcross on her dam's side.

MODERN EUROPEAN KENNELS

In more recent times the German breeder, Frau Vorderstemann, "Heyd-Park" kennel, has owned mostly Tschomo-Lungma stock, but in 1975 she imported a dog from the well-known "Greenmoss" kennel in England. Other present day breeders are Herr Manfred Struve, Lübeck,

"Airs and Graces" kennel, founded in 1971, and Brigitte Niedzwetski's "Tshin-Tamari" kennel, founded in 1982. Frau Reinelt became founder-member of the German Shih Tzu Club in 1982, which gained international status two years later. Until that time the Shih Tzu in Germany had been included in the club for small breeds - the Verband Kleinhundezuchter. An up and coming German kennel is the "Jenshu" kennel of Mr. Jens Niedergessaes, whose DK. Ch. Al Jarreau v. Jenshu, a quality grey/white dog, (who could hold his own anywhere), was best of Breed at Dortmund Ch. Show in 1984 under Mr. Paul Stanton, also Best of Breed at Utrecht, Reeuwarden and the International Shih Tzu Club Show near Hamburg the same year.

Today there are about eleven shows per year in Denmark, with ten to thirty-five entries at each show, some coming from other countries. The top winning Shih Tzu in Denmark in 1982-84 has also been Al Jarreau, now also Lux. and International Champion, top winner at Copenhagen, 1984.

The top winning kennel in Denmark in recent years is "Bain-Zais" owned by A & J Hinløv. This kennel uses old Danish and Dutch (v.d. Oranje Manege) bloodlines, and has made up sixteen Champions during ten years of breeding. The "Gaya" kennel, founded on Ban Zais stock, and owned by K & P Larsen, Rønnede, has won several Best-of-Breeds in 1984 with Gaya's Shu-Shan-Yen.

Frau Puck Vlieghuis-Wijkstra, Slochteren, Holland, has bred many successful Shih Tzus in her "Martinihaim" kennel, including Oruro Tsan, Kyikorien Tsan, and Woekiang Tsan v.h. Martinihaim, who was Best-of-Breed at Arnheim, Eindhoven and Goes (S.W. Holland) in 1984. The sire of Wokiang Tsan was Ch. Oruro Shu v.d. Oranje Manege, who won many titles in the late seventies and has sired numerous winners. The bitch, Ch. Requena Tsan v.h. Martinihaim, red/gold and white, owned my Signora Renata Maraolo, won the title at the F.C.I.'s World Championship Show in Madrid in 1983. The dog title at the Show was won by Ban-Zai's Shu Fy Chiko, black and white, imported into Holland from J. Hindløv in Denmark in 1981 by Mev. Croonenbroek of the "Grunen Gluck" kennel who also owns the International Champion Ban Zai's Shu-Yo-King.

At the International "Winners" Show in Amsterdam, November 1984, the order at the F.C.I.'S Ch. Show the previous year was reversed when the title was won by the dog, Ch. Ben-Zais Shu Fu Chiko, and Best-Opposite-Sex by the bitch, Ch. Requena Tsan v.h. Martinihaim. Signora Maraolo owns a bitch from England, Emrose Saucy Sue, as well as her Martinihaim stock.

In 1973 Mev. Lammers-Schrijver imported the English dog, Whitethroat Ling-tao, into Holland - bred by the late Mrs. Eunice Fox, and sired by Ch. Jen-Kai-Ko of Lhakang ex. Whitethroat Mei-ling. This dog has been used at stud by Mrs. Renzing of the "Klein Oosterling" kennel, and by Mrs. Ebbink of the "Ebbinkshoeve" kennel. Other Dutch breeders are Mijneer v.d. Leeden of the "v.d. Lutine" kennel (who owns the International Champion Ban-Zai's Shu-Ba-Juz) and Peter Burema of the "v.d. Buruf" kennel who has English and Scandinavian stock, which he took over from his mother after her death. Mev. Gayraud owns the "Shaggy Wonder" kennel. Mme. Raedstkarlsson in Belgium breeds and shows "Chicatita" Shih Tzus, and in Denmark Frau Vibeke Vanberg owns the successful "Vibes" kennel.

There are only a few Shih Tzu breeders in France, and the preference is for very small Shih Tzus, sometimes as little as six or seven pounds, (about 2½ - 3½ kilos). Mme. Chantel Mery, Le Vesinet, owns several Champions, including Ch. Muna v. Tschomo-Lungma, a ten-pound black/white bitch from pure Scandinavian bloodlines, who was World Champion in Bern in 1979. Mme. Mery is Vice-President of the French Club (for Tibetan breeds). She owns three out of the thirty surviving pure Scandinavian Shih Tzu - that is, descended from the original three imports in 1932 with no other bloodlines coming in at all. She owns a small stud dog and an 8½ lb. bitch as well as Muna. At the Marseilles International Show in 1984, Mme. Mery's dogs - Ugo, son of Muna and Spoutnik, Utopie and Uddjil "de la Reine Fluerie" were all graded "Excellent" and won top honours, also the "Best-in-Show Breeder's Team".

CH Tragedin Bee Elsudan and his sister CH Teasing Bee Elsudan Born 21.08.82, Breeder / Owner, Danielle Ulrich, France

Now two of them are champions. Mlle. Naudet was one of the first French breeders (together with Mme. Pernier). She acquired a stud dog from Frau Erika Geusendam - Zongo v. Tschomo-Lungma, containing Scandinavian and English blood (from Int. Ch. Hsi-la of Lhakang) and many litters were bred from this stock. Mme Oger started with two English bitches that were bred to dogs belonging to Mme.

Mery and Mme. Ulrich, and she has kept several of the offspring, but seldom manages to attend shows. Mme. J. Bernard obtained her first Shih Tzu from Mrs. Wendy Brown in England and has many other dogs. Mlle. Danielle Ulrich, Normandy, imported Keytor Golden Mist from England in the early 1980's, now an International Champion, and her Elsudan Tragedian Bee (from Greenmoss stock) was Best Junior at the F.C.I. World Championship Show in Madrid in 1983. She has built up her kennel from these two imports. Mme. Reignoux, another French breeder, acquired one of her first Shih Tzus - "Gros Bec Muffin" - from Ireland, and she also owns Greenmoss and Lansu stock from England.

In France, as in other European countries, great emphasis is laid on mouths and an even bite is important. It takes a year to complete the registration of a Shih Tzu with the French Kennel Club, and the mating of sire and dam must be confirmed in writing. The puppies must be registered within fifteen days of birth and at a year old presented to the President of the Breed Society and approved as typical of the breed.

Shih Tzus are still quite rare in Italy: the late Signora Belli was one of the first Shih Tzu owners there. She imported several dogs from England, including Ch. Greenmoss Golden Peregrine of Elfann in the late 1960's and qualified him as an International Champion. This dog contained some of the Scandinavian line through his ancestor, Jungfultets Jung-Ming, imported into England from Sweden in 1959. Signora Belli bred some fine specimens from these imported dogs, but unfortunately after her death her line did not continue. Signora Maraolo, mentioned previously, lives in Milan so the breed has a chance to increase in Italy now.

In Spain the breed is also very rare and the hot dry climate makes it difficult to keep the coat in good condition. David Allan and Javier Bianco breed the "Mimosa" Shih Tzus, and Signora Irene Gomez has stock of English origin, including Fly High of Mimosa Hill, and Mo-Fun of Mimosa Hill, a dog and bitch sired by the famous Int. Ch. Aspen Asian Dandylion. Fly High has been Best-of-Breed several times. Most of the Spanish dogs are gold and white and much smaller than in England. At the 79th International Championship Show in Lisbon in July 1984, multiple B.I.S. Winner Int. Ch. Aspen Asian Dandylion (Mimosa Kennel) bred by Mrs. MacKenzie-Spencer (a well-known Poodle breeder and judge in England), won his Group and went on to win Best-in-Show. At the Madrid Autumn Show, he was Reserve Best-in-Show under Ken Bullock. Dandylion has a promising daughter, Shakarah of Mimosa Hill, who beat her father to Best-of-Breed at the Madrid Spring Show. Sp. Ch. Aspen Jason was exported from England in 1983.

There are very few Shih Tzus known to exist behind the Iron Curtain; however, in 1980, a young Czech, Václav Mazánek, made his presence known by writing to the Manchu Shih Tzu Society in England with a request for literature on the breed. At that time he was the first and only Shih Tzu owner in C.S.S.R. where information on the breed, good breeding stock and grooming equipment were virtually unknown. However he managed to acquire a fine black/white bitch, Etana Chicatita, from Frau Raedts-Karlson in Belgium, who came from Elfann, Lhakang, Lansu, Jungfultets, Orange Manege, Tschomo-Lungma and Bjorneholms bloodlines, thus containing a good variety of English and Scandinavian blood.

Another owner behind the Iron Curtain is Frau Barbara Gollier, who lives in East Germany, a friend of the Mazáneks, who became known to the outside world by writing to the American Shih Tzu Club for information.

Through these contacts and correspondence between owners in other countries, more knowledge was gained about their struggles to establish the breed under difficult conditions. In 1982, the well known

American breeder and judge, Mr. Gilbert Kahn (who owns the Charing Cross Kennel in Florida in partnership with Dr. Jorge Sanchez), visited the Mazáneks in Breclav, Czechoslovakia, and from this visit an exchange of dogs was carried out. Gilbert Kahn chose a black and white bitch puppy Golem Alba, from a current litter and in return sent a handsome young dog, gold, brindle and white, with flowing coat - Charing Cross Prince Andrew. At first Prince Andrew did not settle well; in spite of excellent care he refused to eat or to work at stud, but with veterinary help these problems were overcome and he produced a fine litter of five puppies to Alba's sister.

In 1981 a Shih Tzu Club was started and an All-Breeds Show held in Brno with about 2000 exhibits. In June 1985 Mr Gilbert Kahn was invited to judge the breed at the International Dog Show in Nitra, and Mrs. Gay Widdrington (Lhakang kennel, England) was asked to judge the Czechoslovakian Shih Tzu Club's first Speciality Show held in the historic town of Tabor. The breed has come a long way in Czechoslovakia in five years thanks to the persistence and energy of Mr. Mazánek.

Apart from Denmark, the Scandinavian countries are rabies free so that interchange of dogs and travel to shows held in other European countries is difficult, due to the quarantine regulations. Even so, it can be seen from the above account that Shih Tzus on the Continent come from widely different sources and bloodlines so that variation in type and fashion between one country and another is inevitable, particularly in size and build. We know that the dogs kept in the Imperial Palace, Pekin and the early Scandinavian dogs were of the smaller type, usually under 12 lbs., whilst those imported into the British Isles from China at about the same time, were larger and sturdier - the original three were between 12 - 14½ lbs., with an inclination to increase in size. This might have been due to a more favourable climate and diet, or because some had been bred down from a much larger type of "Lion-dog" which abounded in China outside the Palace.

After World War II, several more bloodlines were imported from China and the strengthening effect of this also tended to produce a larger and more virile dog in the British Isles. For the first two decades the three original imports to Scandinavia were inbred with no other lines coming in, which would tend to reduce size and substance and lead to a more retiring nature. There are still today some of these systematically inbred dogs in European countries. However, all over the world the two basic strains have also been successfully interbred producing many outstanding specimens of beautiful colour combinations.

Breeders in Norway, Sweden and Finland have imported much new stock from the British Isles, successfully incorporating it into their own stock and have now produced some of the most beautiful and typical Shih Tzus to be found anywhere in the world, although with this new blood they have become somewhat larger than the original Scandinavian type. With a wide choice of bloodlines and the many caring and knowledgeable breeders, the Shih Tzu should have a bright future in Europe. But let us hope that their history will be remembered and that the small Palace type will not die out altogether.

In studying the origins of these fascinating dogs, rescued from China only a short time before the breed became extinct there, we must be thankful to those who searched for them so diligently and brought them home to the Western World; one cannot help marvelling at the perils these much-travelled dogs overcame. At the same time it is difficult not to regret the fact that the lines of so many of them did not continue, especially those of M. and Mme. Graeffe's very valuable Palace stock.

CHAPTER 18

STRUCTURE AND MOVEMENT IN THE SHIH TZU
By Tom Horner, 1983

The Shih Tzu has broad resemblances to two other varieties of Eastern dog, in head type, body structure and conformation. Lhasa Apsos are somewhat longer and less square in muzzle, less deep and rounded in body than the Shih Tzu while Pekingese are flatter in face, shorter in neck, lower to ground and markedly more bowed in front with heavier coat and more rounded bodies and their hind legs are held closer together.

In the structure, balance and placement of the limbs there are marked resemblances between the Shih Tzu and the Lhasa Apso with perceptible but not marked differences. The more pronounced features of the Pekingese's structure produce a different type and movement, the greater width of chest and the closer placement of the hind legs producing a pronounced roll in this breed's action.

As in all its features there is nothing over exaggerated about the Shih Tzu's conformation. It should have sufficient length of neck to enable the head to be carried proudly and high, especially on the move, when the desired alert, arrogant and dignified outlook should be in evidence. To secure the right length of neck and high head carriage the shoulders must slope well back. This will ensure the firm level topline with no dip behind the withers (the highest point of the shoulder blades) essential in the Shih Tzu.

Shoulder blades must also slope well back in a correctly formed forehand in this breed - an angle of 45° to the ground is the ideal but a rather greater angle than this will still give sufficient slope. Shoulder blades should slope inwards as well as back, to lie close against the ribcage, any slackness in this area or undue amount of fat under the shoulder blade will lead to a general slackness in the front, and the forelegs turning out of the straight.

The angle at the shoulder joint - where the lower end of the shoulder blade meets the upper end of the humerus or upper arm - should be very pronounced - as near as possible to 90°. With a more open angle at this point the dog's action is bound to be less free i.e. it will step short in front and there may also be looseness at the elbow in pronounced cases. This angulation between the shoulder-blade and the upper arm causes the upper arm to slope backwards along the chest wall and places the elbow well back from the front of the chest - i.e. well under the dog, and so in a position to support the heavy body and head of the dog.

Elbows must be well tucked in to the dog's body, the floor of the chest should reach down to the level of the elbow in this breed, but the elbows must also be free to move to and fro as the dog extends its forelegs. If they are tied in too tight the dog will turn its toes outward as it moves. As in all low to ground breeds there is a slight curve in the bone of the foreleg down to the wrist. It follows the curve of the slightly rounded ribs. The heavy coat on the forelegs hides this curve from sight, but it is there as will be revealed by careful handling.

Below the wrist - the joint between the forearm (the ulna/radius) and the pastern -, the feet should point straight forward. The distance between the forelegs and feet depends on the width of the chest, it will be found that some strongly built males with rather over rounded ribs tend to roll from side to side as they move, seldom seen in the more finely build females. This broad chest of the Pekingese coupled with the pronounced bend in the forelegs and the close hind movement produces the Pekingese roll.

In movement the Shih Tzu forelegs should remain parallel, even at fast speeds. If it tends to turn its toes in or move with one foot in front of the other - single tracking - it will be found that there is a flaw in the conformation of its forehand - it may be too fat pushing out its elbows, too short and/or steep in upper arm, or that there is insufficient slope at the shoulder; or the dog may be nervous or badly handled - on too tight a lead. A properly made fit and confident Shih Tzu should always move with the forelegs in parallel. This breed should be moved at a pace that best displays its outline, head carriage and natural self esteem - not rushed around the ring at the speed of a long legged breed.

Common faults in the forehand of the Shih Tzu, which are inevitably transmitted to its movement are protruding elbows, usually caused by upright shoulders and/or short steep upper arms, soft flat feet and weak pasterns. Breeding for better conformation will rectify most of them, but it may take time.

THE HINDQUARTERS

To secure the unique flowing, driving hind action of the Shih Tzu the conformation of the body, including the loins and the croup, and of the hindquarters must be about right and the dog must receive sufficient exercise to give tone to the muscles, hind action and conformation at the rear of this breed. The Lhasa Apso are very similar. A level topline stemming from well placed shoulders, a short strong loin and a correctly placed croup to give the desired high set tail are more frequently seen in the Shih Tzu than is the correct forehand conformation.

These factors are all necessary to secure correct hind movement but must be allied with short hocks - not too far from the ground - and well turned stifles. Well turned stifles come about only when there is sufficient length in the femur - the upper thigh and the tibia/fibula, the lower thigh, to form almost a right angle at the stifle joint. Well angulated stifles are an absolute essential for sound flowing movement with the desired drive in short legged breeds.

From behind, the Shih Tzu should show pronounced drive and flowing movement. There should be no trace of jerking or undue up and down movement of the hocks as sometimes seen in the Lhasa Apso. The pads of the feet should show and the legs remain always parallel, even at fast paces. Well developed muscles are vital to produce the desired drive in the Shih Tzu's hind movement.

Cow hocks, bowed hocks and moving close are all faults that arise from poor structure in the hind legs. The length of one hock - back pastern - is a good width between the hocks. This gives a balanced look to the moving dog - neither too close nor too far apart. When hocks and/or stifles are too straight the above mentioned faults tend to arise and are difficult to breed out except by use of exceptionally well built partners.

Straight stifles and hocks can also cause the topline to run up towards the set of the tail. One should always test for this with the hand as an unduly thick coat can give the impression of running up which may not be the case. A roach back, a very bad fault in the Shih Tzu, can be camouflaged by clever grooming and judges need to use their hands on this breed to secure a proper assessment.

Movement in the Shih Tzu should always be assessed from three directions - moving across the judge's line of sight, as when moving round the show ring, going away and coming towards the judge - in each of the two latter directions it is essential to see the dog moved in a straight line. The triangle, properly used, is a most useful device for the assessment of movement in this breed.

Moving round the ring the Shih Tzu should be seen to hold its head high, its topline level with the tail well over the back, to stride out freely in front with good length of stride and no apparent effort or difficulty and no undue lifting of the forefeet. The hind legs should be brought well forward under the body without undue lift and should extend well out behind the dog without any trace of exaggerated thrust or lift. The whole dog should flow round the ring with pride and arrogance in his style, forelegs and hind legs in complete co-ordination, a level topline, tail on high as if he owned the world and wished everyone to know it.

Coming towards the judge the high head carriage should be maintained along with the proud bearing and the forelegs reaching well forward, remaining in parallel, so long as the dog is moved at a sensible speed.

Going away the head should still be held high, the tail well up, the backline level and the hind legs exhibiting the so-desired flowing drive. Even the dogs' pads have a look of arrogance about them as they move away remaining always in parallel.

Celestial Happy Land, Sheila Bode

<u>Bibliography</u>

1) VWF Collier, "Dogs of China and Japan in Nature and Art", Wm Heineman, London.
(See Chapter XII and illustrations on p. 182).

2) "The Lion Dog of Pekin" A C Dixey, Peter Davies Ltd, London, 1931.
About the Pekingese, but useful information on the cult of the Lion Dog, and some mention of the Shih Tzu type.

3) "Chinese Pottery in the Han Dynasty" Barthold Laufer, CE Tuttle & Co. Inc Rutland, Vermont and Tokyo, Japan.
(Useful early background information and mention of tribute dogs.) 1962.

4) "Hutchinson's Popular & Ilustrated Dog Encyclopaedia Vol II Edited by Walter Hutchinson. Hutchinson and Co, London. Probably published in 1930's.
Many photographs of early dogs and write-up of breed. Describes original mix-up between Shih Tzus and Apsos.

5) "Chinese Creeds and Customs. Vol III" by VR Burkhardt. South China Morning Post, Hong Kong 1958.
(See p 87 Write-up, Breed and etching.)

6) "Imperial Incense" by Princess Der Ling. Stanley Paul & Co Ltd, London.
Chapter on Royal Kennels" with mention of Shih Tzu type. Not dated, but dedicated to her son and so probably later than below.

7) "Two Years in the Forbidden City" Princess Der Ling. T Fisher Unwin, London and Leipsic 1912.
Fascinating background information and illustrations of court life.

8) "A Dream of Tartary" The origins and misfortunes of Henry P'U Yi, last Emperor of China. Geo Allen and Unwin Ltd London 1963.
Useful background information, but no mention of dogs.

Gay Widdrington in 1967 with L. Sing-Hi of Lhakang and his son, Int. Ch. Greenmoss Golden Peregrine of Elfann.